MAKING YOUR MARRIAGE
A LOVE STORY

DR. C. THOMAS AND
PASTOR MAUREEN ANDERSON

WITH
DON ENEVOLDSEN

WINWORD
PUBLISHING

Phoenix, Arizona

FIRST EDITION

Published by **Winword Publishing, Inc.**
3520 E. Brown Road, Mesa, AZ 85213
(480) 964-4GOD

ISBN 1-58588-012-4

Office number for book orders:

1-888-4WORDTV (1-888-496-7388), ext. 118

or visit **www.winners.tv**

CONTENTS

ONCE UPON A TIME

Personal Story: Tom

Our marriage has had many of the misunder-standings and miscommunications that make a love story. The amazing part of it all is that God was able to get us together anyway. Even before we were engaged you could see God working around our own blunderings.

I was in the United States Navy, stationed in Naples, Italy, when I got a letter from Maureen that she would like to have me take her to the Junior Prom. I didn't have any money, so I borrowed eleven hundred dollars from American Express, back in 1963, and I flew to Rome, from Rome to New York, then to Minneapolis and from there I took a bus home. I took her to the prom, got back on the bus, rode back to Minneapolis and on to New York. I missed my flight from New York, took a later flight to Rome and rode the train back to Naples. As soon as I arrived the Shore Patrol arrested me because my ship had pulled out and, because of the late flight from New York, I missed it. So I was held in Naples for twenty-eight days until my ship came back. By the time I got to the ship I had a "Dear John" letter from Maureen. She actually broke up with me right after the prom.

It took me two years to pay off the loan from American Express.

Personal Story: Maureen

I was going with a boy in my class and he was going to be the prom king, which meant that he would choose the prom queen. He was very popular but a few months before the election for the prom he had taken out another girl. He called me to say he was sorry. The other guys had talked him into it and he was really sorry.

But I just told him, "Forget it. I don't like you anyway. And I don't want to date you." I said it because I was mad and hurt.

But then I realized that I wouldn't have a date to the prom. So I sent a letter to Tom and told him that the prom was coming up and I wanted to go with him. He came home and after he left I sent him a letter saying that I didn't want to be dating him. He was just too wild for me.

Personal Story: Tom

Just before I got out of the service I decided that I had been through enough. Maureen and I had been dating off and on for a number of years and the pain just seemed like too much. So I decided to write her a letter and tell her I was all done with her. Forget it. I was going on with my life. I told her I was dating someone else and I didn't want to see her again.

I guess it was probably a week and a half later that we were steaming somewhere off the shores of Malta in the Mediterranean when I got an emergency phone call. Of course my first thought was that my family had all been killed or something traumatic. You just never get phone calls, especially at sea. There were no satellites so it was a very difficult thing to patch a call through.

I ran up to the bridge and into the IC room, put on the head set and said, "Hello." This little voice on the other end said, "Hi, Tom." It was Maureen. I couldn't believe my ears. In fact the IC fellow flipped on the switch so that the entire ship listened to our conversation. Three hundred men throughout the entire ship. I didn't know that until afterwards.

Personal Story: Maureen

Well, after I graduated from high school I dated several guys. This one boy was the son of a Baptist preacher, a really nice guy, going to college and all. He had been very upset with me. He wrote a letter explaining that he was upset because I was always late. He said that he had even been thinking about marrying me.

I was nineteen at the time and I suddenly realized that this was serious. So I prayed. I didn't know God at the time and I didn't go to church but I still had a relationship with God in the sense that I didn't want to do anything wrong or anything that would hurt Him, so I prayed, "God, who should I marry?"

Right inside of me I heard a voice that said, "Tom." So that settled it.

Then the next morning I went to the mail box and there was a letter from Tom saying that he was getting out of the service, that he was dating someone else and that he never wanted to see me again. He was done. He didn't want to go through the pain anymore.

I was in a panic. I felt I just had to call him right away. I went to the phone and I called the Navy and said, "This is an emergency. I've got to talk to Carl Anderson now."

They didn't even ask me why. They just said, "Okay," and they began to go from ship to ship until I was able to apologize and say I was sorry and that I hoped we could have a relationship.

And Tom just melted and that was it. We got married a year later.

Personal Story: Tom

*I think that the most amazing thing is that nei-
ther one of us was born again, but God had a plan.
Maureen called the United States Navy and asked
for Carl Anderson and they patched it through from
Norfolk, Virginia. The only way you could get across
the sea was from ship to ship, each of which had a
range of about three hundred miles. All of the people
along the way had to be willing to do this and then
to connect them all the way to the middle of the Mediterranean and be able to hear clear as a bell. That
was an amazing thing. I don't know how many ships
and people listened to our conversation and how
many might still be talking about that strange phone
call. Only God could have put that together.*

Everyone loves a love story. The joy, the pain, the struggles and the happy ending touch the emotions of every per-son alive. We identify with the feelings of love at some level, either through our own experience or, more often, through the longing for feelings of romance that we don't have but which we believe are the best part of life.

The names most indelibly etched in our memory are couples who lived out a passion beyond the normal scope of everyday life, and that passion, whether "good" or "tragic," makes them memorable. Certain names are forever spoken in unison because we cannot, or perhaps do not want to, separate them — Romeo and Juliet, Samson and Delilah, David and Bathsheba, Napoleon and Josephine, Ozzie and Harriet. The relationships are not always healthy. In fact they usually are not, but the passion they exude creates an excitement we do not often see in our own lives. It is rare to encounter a novel, a movie, a play, a television show or a song without a "love interest." We live for love.

Love stories don't just happen. They are created.

Against this backdrop our own lives often seem remarkably mundane. Our personal love stories are more often years of boredom punctuated with brief moments of ecstasy. Courtship and marriage are exciting as we fall into the emotions of love but once the wedding is finished the routine of life takes over and we begin to think that something is wrong.

This craving for stories of love is not accidental. God created human beings to need the exciting elements of a love story. What is wrong is the manner in which we expect the emotions to come to us. The emotion of love is not a feeling that comes and goes without warning or without reason. It is the outgrowth of effort, of communication and of learning to serve one another. Love stories don't just happen. They are created. It is God's desire that every marriage be a love story, but without some work it will be nothing more than a desire.

Good love stories have certain characteristics that are

consistent through time and culture. In the stories that move us, two people come together with needs that are met only in each other. They make mistakes along the way. There is conflict, often because of a breakdown in communication. There is opposition to the relationship, factors that threaten to destroy it.

But the two love each other so much that they allow nothing to stand in the way. They sacrifice all to satisfy each other's needs. They overcome every obstacle to be together. They resolve every conflict and forgive every wrong.

A good love story is not without conflict and trial. But the happy ending is worth the effort. We all want to "live happily ever after."

God gave marriage to the church. It is a gift. The greatest love story of all is His love for His people. From beginning to end the Bible portrays God's love in the terms of a marriage. It is a picture that permeates the imagery of prophetic scripture. The parable of the foolish and the wise virgins, for example, is set in a wedding. The words of Jesus concerning when he would return are part of the old Jewish wedding rituals.

> *But of that day and hour no one*
> *knows, not even the angels of heaven, but*
> *My Father only.* (Matthew 24:36)

When Jesus said these words He was referring directly to marriage. In the time of Christ, when a young Jewish man wanted to marry a girl, he first approached her father carrying a flask of wine and a marriage contract that spelled out all the promises he would make to her and how he intended to support her. Once the father agreed to the contract they sealed it by sharing a glass of wine. The prospective groom then poured another glass of the wine and set it on the table while the girl was called into the room.

If she agreed to the marriage she indicated it by drinking from the glass. From that moment on the two were considered to be bound by contract and a divorce was required to break the engagement. The groom returned to his father's home where he began preparing for the wedding by constructing a house for his new wife. He could not return for his bride until his father approved of the construction. If anyone asked him when the wedding would take place he replied, "No one knows the time but my father."

When approval was finally given, the groom sent two of his friends to bring the bride back for the wedding feast which usually lasted for seven days. During that time the bride and groom consummated the marriage.

The parallel is obvious. Jesus, the groom, proposed marriage to his bride, the church. The marriage contract that spelled out His promises and how He would provide for her is his Word. Every time the bride drinks the wine of communion she is reaffirming her acceptance of His proposal. Jesus has gone back to his Father and is preparing a home for His bride. When the Father says it is ready, then Jesus will send for His bride and the marriage feast will begin.

Marriage is a picture of this relationship and it is a love story in every sense of the word. The story has conflicts and misunderstandings, breakdowns in communication and resistance to the relationship. But the perfect groom overcomes all obstacles, even sacrificing himself so that nothing will stand between him and the object of his love.

We want to take you through the love story of the Bible. We want you to see and experience the principles that will make your marriage exciting, healthy and fulfilling. Conflict does not have to be the norm but to be rid of it you will have to overcome every obstacle in yourself that keeps you from a healthy marriage. You will need to change how you think and how you act.

The perfect groom overcomes all obstacles, even sacrificing himself.

We will focus on the one book of the Bible that is entirely devoted to romantic love — the Song of Solomon. It is a love song, a story of emotion, of overwhelming need and selfless fulfillment, of romance, of sensual and erotic passion. Like every good love story it has conflict and tension, resolution and a happy ending. We will see that the lovers of Solomon's song were not much different than you and I. When we are done you will not only see that your marriage can work, but it can become a moving, exciting and dynamic love story in its own right.

*The argument you
just won with your
wife isn't over yet.*

12 MAKING YOUR MARRIAGE A LOVE STORY

1

𝕾

MACHOISM VS. FEMINISM
EQUALITY IN LOVE

A garden enclosed
Is my sister, my spouse,
A spring shut up,
A fountain sealed.
(Song of Solomon 4:12)

T he roles of husband and wife are hinted at by illustration in many places in the Song of Solomon. The husband as a protector is portrayed by his strength.

The picture of the bride as an enclosed garden is not intended to be a restrictive image. Rather, it expresses the groom's perception of her as living and growing. He declares that he will provide an environment in which she can flourish like a garden, growing to her fullest potential.

For her part the bride meets the needs of her husband. She describes herself in terms of pleasing him.

Then I became in his eyes
As one who found peace.
(Song of Solomon 8:10)

The New International Version translates it as "I have become in his eyes as one who brings contentment." The

Garden of Eden gives us a picture of the interplay of responsibility between husband and wife. The first thing we see is that God created Adam and Eve to be equals.

> *So God created man in His own image; in the image of God He created him; male and female He created them.* (Genesis 1:27)

In history it has been taught by the church that men are made in the image of God and women are somehow inferior, as though they are only partly made in God's image. Augustine, for example, claimed that man, but not woman, was made in God's image and therefore woman is not complete without man but man is complete alone.

Yet Genesis says specifically that both male and female are created in his image. We call God our Father, but he is also *El Shaddai,* the many-breasted one. He has some characteristics that are masculine and other characteristics that are feminine. He can be a husband to the husbandless and a wife to the wifeless. Both male and female are in God's image. He has given the same authority to both. In verse 28 God blessed "them," both of them, not just the man.

Both Adam and Eve were given dominion. Both were supposed to subdue the earth. Both were to be fruitful and multiply. Both had authority and both had responsibility. Both were equal before God.

Because both had authority we need to recognize the

absurdity of some of our past beliefs about marriage. Is it wrong for a wife to work, for example?

The virtuous woman described in Proverbs 31 certainly did. She bought a field. She planted a vineyard. She worked late into the night. She bought and sold goods. She invested money. She managed servants. She worked.

This does not mean a woman should not take time off from work when her children are young so that she can be with them. But it does mean God is not bothered by women with jobs and careers outside the home.

> *God created Adam and Eve to be equals.*

The creation of Eve emphasized the equality of man and woman. When Adam first appeared on the earth he was both Adam and Eve. She was taken from him.

We have some pleasant little teachings about the rib that tell us Eve was taken from under Adam's arm so that she would be protected, not from his head lest she dominate him and not from his foot lest he walk on her. These stories make us feel good but they are not entirely accurate.

The Hebrew word translated "rib" is *tsela'*. It literally means "half." It is used to describe half a hill or half the Tabernacle. God divided Adam in two.

One half was then Adam and the other half He turned into Eve. Adam was never whole again without Eve. Husband and wife together make a complete unit.

That unit is truly the image of God. There was only

one thing in all creation that God said was not good. And that was the fact that the man was alone.

> And the LORD God said, "It is not good
> that man should be alone; I will make him
> a helper comparable to him." (Genesis
> 2:18)

The question we need to ask is, "Why was it not good for the man to be alone?"

Most people answer that question from a self-centered perspective. "It was not good because Adam was lonely." But God never approaches anything from a selfish perspective.

The truth is that God is very interested in the interaction and self-sacrifice of relationship. He is Himself three persons — Father, Son and Spirit — each in complete submission to the other two and all three equal. Each lays His life down in service to the others. Because of this, God is one, in perfect harmony.

Man cannot live fully in God's image until he is laying his life down in service to others. This character trait is so much a part of God's image and His personality that man, made in God's image, cannot be content until he serves. It was not good for Adam to be alone because, while he was alone, there was no one to serve.

So God's plan was for husband and wife to be equal, even though they were different. Each had strengths unique to them. Each had a role to play in the marriage. The original sin in the garden was not just because of Eve's mistake. It resulted from both husband and wife failing to accept the responsibilities of their roles in the marriage.

When we look at the incident in the Garden it appears that Adam was not listening. Eve may have been talking but he was not hearing anything she said. He was there through the whole thing. The Bible makes that clear.

She also gave to her husband with her,
and he ate. (Genesis 3:6)

As the responsible party it was his job to protect Eve. But he wasn't even paying attention. Like many men, he was passive. He didn't want to rock the boat or say anything confrontational — peace at any cost. If he had been acting as the responsible party he would have realized his wife was talking to a snake. He would have spoken up when he heard what the snake had to say and he would have refuted it. Adam chose to eat along with Eve rather than risk disagreement. He chose to join her rather than protect her.

Eve, on the other hand, if she understood how submission worked, would have gone to Adam and asked him about what the snake had to say. At his very first words she would have sought her husband's advice. She would have made Adam take the responsibility.

But like many women, when her husband wasn't paying attention, she sought conversation elsewhere. At least the snake listened. And not just one time. It was not a matter of walking up to the serpent, hearing a few comments and eating the fruit. The Hebrew verbs used in this passage indicate that Eve and the serpent had an ongoing conversation. She heard him continually, day after day, over an extended period of time.

Faith comes the same way. It is built by repetition, by hearing and hearing and hearing the Word. This is the meaning of the Greek words in Romans 10:17. If you listen to something long enough it will become part of your belief system.

So Eve listened every day. She kept coming back. What did she hear? "This fruit is good. God didn't really want you to stay away from it. You just didn't understand Him. He doesn't want you to be like Him."

All the time the devil was trying to bring separation. When Adam and Eve were one with each other there was the power of agreement. Each submitted to the other. Each protected the other. Each contributed to the health and success of the marriage. When they acted on their own, they got into trouble.

It is with Adam eating the fruit that we really see the role of the husband as the responsible party. Eve ate and nothing happened. Nothing changed. It was only after Adam came into agreement with Eve and ate that they became aware.

She also gave to her husband with her,
and he ate. Then the eyes of both of them
were opened. . . (Genesis 3:6-7)

In other words, if Adam had not eaten, Eve would have been protected. Being the head of the house does not mean domination by force. Adam did not have to force Eve to avoid the fruit. He did not have to beat her every time she talked to the snake. All he had to do was take a stand and refuse to agree with her actions and she would have been covered. Unfortunately that's something he did not do.

Adam's position as the responsible party was a direct result of how God created him. He was different than Eve. That does not mean he was superior to her, just different. Men and women are not the same.

When Adam and Eve were one with each other, there was the power of agreement.

In 1987 Dr. Sperry conducted some research concerning the mental development of unborn children. His findings showed that between the 22nd and the 25th week of gestation a chemical is injected into the brain of the male fetus that inhibits the growth of the emotional side of the brain and enhances the growth of the logical side.

As a result men and women have brains that work differently from each other. Men are more logical. Women are more emotional.

This does not mean that men are not emotional. Neither does it mean that women are not logical. But the structure of their brains does create a significant difference. Another way of saying it is that men are more logical and women are more intuitive. Either trait can be a strength in the right circumstances. But each can be a weakness, too.

In the spiritual realm this difference causes men and women to react differently to spiritual things. In the ministry we have had opportunity to see people react to God in many ways. Women have a tendency to be more open to all that the spirit of God has than men are. But they also have a tendency to rush in without checking the validity of the experience.

It is much like jumping off the end of a pier into the water. Women like to run off the end of the dock and be instantly immersed in all that God has. They don't check to see how deep the water is. They don't care whether it's hot or cold. None of that matters.

Men, on the other hand, tend to walk down the dock, put their foot in, evaluate it to see if it is safe or not. Only then do they ease themselves in.

Neither way is right or wrong by itself. God intended that husband and wife work together. Her intuitive nature should help him move along faster. His logic should protect her from getting into water where she will be hurt.

The husband is the responsible party because of his logic, not because of any superiority. God intended husband and wife to be equal partners, walking together side by side in a harmony of purpose.

*After winning an
argument with
his wife,
the wisest thing
a man can do
is apologize.*

2

SUBMIT ONLY TO LOVE
BIBLICAL ORDER IN MARRIAGE

Oh, that you were like my brother,
Who nursed at my mother's breasts!
If I should find you outside,
I would kiss you;
I would not be despised.
I would lead you and bring you
Into the house of my mother,
She who used to instruct me.
I would cause you to drink of spiced wine,
Of the juice of my pomegranate.
(Song of Solomon 8:1-2)

The Song of Solomon has several voices who speak in different parts of the poem. A kind of chorus, for example, is provided by a group referred to as the "friends of the bride" or the "daughters of Jerusalem." Others may be present as well but the majority of the poem, about 92 percent of the total text, is divided between the bride and the bridegroom.

When we examine what each says it is interesting to note how much of the conversation is from the bride. Bible scholars A. LaCocque and S. D. Goitein point out that the bride speaks 53 percent of the time compared with only 39 percent for the groom. It is not the amount of talking the bride does that is most noteworthy, however. It is the aggressiveness she displays.

This passage in 8:1-2, for example, is one of several that show the woman initiating the encounter. She not only initiates but demonstrates that she would not hold back even in a public place. She would pursue her man even with others watching. Her aggressiveness throughout the book runs contrary to traditional stereotypes of how godly women should act. Obviously the biblical idea of submission does not mean subservience.

> *Obviously the biblical idea of submission does not mean subservience.*

As we study what submission really means, we will see that the bride is very much submitted to the groom.

> *I am my beloved's,*
> *And his desire is toward me.*
> (Song of Solomon 7:10)

She is submitted to him but he does not control her. Rather there is a mutual submission to each other.

> *I am my beloved's*
> *And my beloved is mine.*
> (Song of Solomon 6:3)

Her submission is a response to his love, not a response to his power or even to his position.

> *He brought me to the banqueting house,*
> *And his banner over me was love.*
> (Song of Solomon 2:4)

Over the years the church has used scripture to control women, to keep them in their place and keep them quiet. To do that requires looking at only a few verses and ignoring many others.

Ephesians 5:22, for example, has been quoted over and over to justify husbands controlling their wives, to feeling elite or superior to them.

> *Wives, submit to your own husbands,*
> *as to the Lord.* (Ephesians 5:22)

Taken completely out of context this verse says simply, "Wives submit." But that phrase, by itself, is not the whole picture. Too many people forget the last part which says, "as to the Lord." They believe that submitting to a husband means submitting to his junk.

But if you're only going to submit as you would to the Lord,

If you're only going to submit as you would to the Lord, then you are only going to submit to love.

then you are only going to submit to love — never to abuse, never to hurt, never to pain and especially never to sin. God would not ask anyone to submit to sin. We have ignored a significant part of Paul's words.

The words that precede verse 22 are just as important as those that follow. In most Bibles, verse 21 is separated from verse 22 by a heading or at least a new paragraph. In the original manuscripts, however, there was no break at all. If any break was intended it would be at verse 20. Paul often concluded a thought with comments like this one.

Giving thanks always for all things to
God the Father in the name of our Lord
Jesus Christ. (Ephesians 5:20)

Usually this kind of a statement ends the thought and indicates a new paragraph. This means that the direction for wives to submit to their husbands is prefaced with a more all-inclusive command. Literally it would read more like this.

Submitting to one another in the fear
of God, wives, submit to your own hus-
bands, as to the Lord.

Love involves the body of Christ learning to submit to one another. It's about both husband and wife learning to submit. It means submitting to love and to nothing else. Paul states it even more plainly in his letter to the Corinthians.

> *The wife does not have authority over her own body, but the husband does. And likewise the husband does not have authority over his own body, but the wife does.* (1 Corinthians 7:4)

We only submit to love. If the body of Christ could only understand this they wouldn't end up in Guyana drinking "Kool Aid." And spousal abuse would not be tolerated by the church.

The context of Paul's comments on submission makes it clear that God never intended for women to be subjected to the domination of their husbands. They are to be subject to his love. When the next few verses are added the picture is even clearer.

> *For the husband is head of the wife, as also Christ is head of the church; and He is the Savior of the body. Therefore, just as the church is subject to Christ, so let the wives be to their own husbands in everything.* (Ephesians 5:23-24)

Jesus, as the savior of the body, actually died for the church. The same responsibility, then, is incumbent on the husband, that is, he is expected to give up his life for the good of his wife, to lay down his own desires for the welfare of his family.

This is the relationship in which the church is subject to Christ. The wife is never instructed to submit to any other kind of relationship than one based on the same kind of love.

Smith Wigglesworth was one of the most powerful men of God who ever lived. He told the story of how his wife stood up to him and refused to obey him. At one point in his life he became a workaholic. Working seven days a week he gradually became very indifferent and even hostile to church. His wife still attended regularly and it began to irritate him.

He told her, "You go to church too much. You're not to go any more. I know enough about the Bible to know the man is the head of the wife. You're to obey me. And I say, 'Don't go to church,' so you're not going."

She refused to submit to his junk. She just smiled and said, "Now, Smith, you're the head of this house, and you're my husband. Whatever you say in the house goes. And you know as well as I do that I do not neglect you, the children, or the house in any way. But you are not my lord. Jesus is my Lord. And the Bible tells us not to forsake the assembling of ourselves together. The Bible tells me to go to church, and I'm going."

He did his best to intimidate her. It made no difference. He described the results in these words. "Well, I'd fume and fuss and practically cuss. And finally one day I told her, 'If you go tonight — I'll lock you out.' But she went right along — and I locked her out. She didn't have a key and couldn't get in. The next morning I came downstairs, opened the back door, and there she was, all bundled up in her coat, leaning up against the door. She had been there all night. When I opened the door, she almost fell into the kitchen. But she bounded up, smiled, and said, 'Well, dear, how are you this morning?'

"She was so kind and sweet, but I'd have felt better if she'd chewed on me a little. She didn't, though. She just asked, 'What would you like for breakfast?' And she fixed my favorite breakfast.

─────── ℘ ───────

Marriage is not about who is in charge. It is about responsibility.

─────────────

" 'All right, all right,' I said, 'I'm wrong. I missed it.' She had just loved me back to God. But at the same time, she stood her ground. If she had quit church and followed me, we'd have both been in trouble."

Marriage is not about who is in charge. It is about responsibility. It is a fifty/fifty partnership in which both the husband and the wife have a God-given responsibility. The husband's responsibility is to be the head of the house.

But the emphasis should be on the responsibility, not on the privilege or power. He is the responsible party, which means his wife's welfare reflects on him. Part of the responsibility that Jesus accepted in his relationship with the church was to sanctify the church, to cleanse her, to set her apart as holy so that she will be without spot or blemish.

> *Husbands, love your wives, just as*
> *Christ also loved the church and gave*

Himself up for her, that He might sanctify and cleanse her with the washing of water by the word, that He might present her to Himself a glorious church, not having spot or wrinkle or any such thing, but that she should be holy and without blemish. (Ephesians 5:25-27)

The same is true of the husband's responsibility. He is to set his wife apart in his own thinking in such a way that he seeks to wash her with the water of the Word. That means he spends time speaking the promises of the Word of God over her and doing all that he can to help her fulfill her destiny.

Most women did not marry their husband because they loved him. They married him because he loved them.

If a husband is smart enough he will realize that the Bible says wisdom is on a wife's tongue (Proverbs 31:26). He could learn some things. He accepts the responsibility for the decision making but he only makes decisions based on what is best for his wife and his children. Ephesians is not about domination or power. It is about responsibility, and responsibility is about giving, not getting. In fact, the husband who loves his wife loves himself.

Jesus was not concerned about how much the cross would hurt. He wasn't concerned with the thorns. He wasn't concerned about going to the grave. His only concern was for what would be best for the bride. Most women did not marry their husband because they loved him. They married him because he loved them.

This does not mean a husband should just lie down and let his wife wipe her feet on him. That's not the point. The wife has a responsibility to love him in return. But God has made the husband the responsible party.

An understanding of these few verses in Ephesians would heal most problems in most marriages. A husband who learns to love his wife will find that she will gladly submit herself to his love. A wife who learns to love her husband will encourage him by her words and actions. She will send him off every day to conquer the world. When she does that he will do virtually anything to please her. The husband has an innate desire to please his wife because she is the only one who can truly please him.

*When a girl
marries, she gives
up the attention
of many men
for the
inattentiveness
of one.*

3

☙

I LOVE YOU! PROVE IT!
THE EXPRESSION OF LOVE

Let me hear your voice;
For your voice is sweet,
And your face is lovely.
(Song of Solomon 2:14)

When reading the Song of Solomon, one is struck by the range of expression used by the lovers. Every expression common to romance is demonstrated at some point. In this verse we see the communication of love through words. "Let me hear your voice," the bride says. In fact it is the groom's voice that first catches her attention.

The voice of my beloved!
Behold, he comes
Leaping upon the mountains,
Skipping upon the hills.
(Song of Solomon 2:8)

Being a poem, the Song of Solomon gives numerous examples of speech designed to say "love" — compliments, affirmation and encouragement. Seeing the face is not enough. The bride needs to hear her lover's voice as well. In numerous places he responds with praise.

Behold, you are fair, my love!
Behold, you are fair!
You have dove's eyes behind your veil.
Your hair is like a flock of goats,
Going down from Mount Gilead.
Your teeth are like a flock of shorn sheep
Which have come up from the washing,
Every one of which bears twins,
And none is barren among them.
Your lips are like a strand of scarlet,
And your mouth is lovely.
Your temples behind your veil
Are like a piece of pomegranate.
                    (Song of Solomon 4:1-3)

Words are the most prominent way that love is expressed, which is to be expected since it is a poem, but the Song of Solomon portrays several other types of expression as well. The groom, for example, gives generously of his possessions.

Follow in the footsteps of the flock,
And feed your little goats
Beside the shepherd's tents.
                    (Song of Solomon 1:8)

The bride also gives to him.

> *Let my beloved come to his garden*
> *And eat its pleasant fruits.*
>   (Song of Solomon 4:16)

Even the friends play a part.

> *We will make you ornaments of gold*
> *With studs of silver.*
>   (Song of Solomon 1:11)

The physical aspects of love are obvious in the dialogue between the lovers.

> *I held him and would not let him go.*
>   (Song of Solomon 3:4)

Much of the imagery is clearly referring to sexual love.

> *His left hand is under my head,*
> *And his right hand embraces me.*
>   (Song of Solomon 8:3)

Love is expressed by the actions of the lovers, the things they do for each other.

> *Sustain me with cakes of raisins,*
> *Refresh me with apples.*
>   (Song of Solomon 2:5)

It is also expressed in the desire to spend time with each other.

Come, my beloved,
Let us go forth to the field;
Let us lodge in the villages.
Let us get up early to the vineyards;
Let us see if the vine has budded,
Whether the grape blossoms are open,
And the pomegranates are in bloom.
(Song of Solomon 7:11-12)

The bride and the groom in the Song of Solomon are obviously very much in love with each other and they strive to express that love in a variety of ways. The expression of love is what reinforces the reality of love. Love needs expression.

These various expressions of love are defined by Gary Chapman in his book *The Five Love Languages*. He calls them "words of affirmation," "gift giving," "physical touch and closeness," "acts of service," and "quality time." Each is a kind of language and each is different.

> *The expression of love is what reinforces the reality of love.*

Chapman has identified a very basic need in every person to have love expressed to them. Without receiving an appropriate expression of love we feel empty and insecure.

When the need for an expression of love is met, we experience fulfillment and a sense of security.

The problem with expression is that different people respond differently to various expressions. Some people feel loved when their mate brings them gifts. Some feel loved when their mate spends time with them. Others feel loved when their mate compliments and encourages them. Speak to them in a love language that they do not respond to and the need for love is not met. It's like trying to talk to them in a foreign language.

A significant part of learning to communicate in a marriage is learning how your mate receives love so that you can adapt your expression to them. Most people tend to express love in the same way that they want it expressed to them and that isn't always the best way.

Personal Story: Maureen

I came from a home that was big. I had four brothers and there was always a lot of movement going on, a lot of activity. Everybody was doing their own thing in my family. Independence. If you wanted a meal you cooked it. If you wanted your clothes washed you washed them. We all just fended for ourselves.

But we would sit at the table and we would talk for a couple of hours. So we had a very talkative family, a big family and a lot of noise. And that's how I received love, through encouraging words and quality time.

Tom came from a small family. He was the only child until he was eleven years old. His step-mother came from Norway and she could hardly speak any English. So he came from a very quiet home. His mother never said, "I love you," but instead she waited on him hand and foot. She didn't even sit down and eat a meal. She waited on everybody at the table and that's how she expressed love. That's how Tom was raised and that's how he received love.

So we get married and Tom comes home from work and I have the table set and we're eating. And Tom says, "I'd like some ketchup."

Well, in my home, if you wanted ketchup you got up and got it, so I'm thinking to myself, "Why is he asking me? I don't want ketchup. He wants ketchup." So, being a sweet, new bride, I said, "Honey, it's in the refrigerator." Of course, he receives love through those actions of service. So I have just denied him love.

Now, in my family we sat and talked for a couple of hours. That's how I receive love. But I wasn't even done eating and he was gone. He was off doing something else and I wanted to talk.

We were speaking to each other in the wrong love language. I needed to hear affirming words but he was waiting on me. He needed to be waited on but I was speaking affirming words to him. We had to learn to express love in the right language.

ॐ

Affirming words are those that build someone up. People whose primary love language is encouraging words need to hear their mate speak. Such words give a verbal appreciation for what the other person does. They give compliments.

You need to expand your vocabulary of compliments so that you can verbally pat your mate on the back. Statements like, "I admire you, I adore you, I cherish you, you are beautiful, you mean everything to me," will build up your mate. They are words that create life. Every time your mate does something good, give a compliment. They bring out the untapped potential in different areas of his or her life.

Affirming words are always positive. Don't nag. Forget about little things that don't matter. Learn to compliment. For many people, learning to speak encouraging words can be sacrificial. But a person who receives love through words can be very sensitive about words. They often get hurt easily because words are so important to them. You need to learn what is important to your spouse and give them praise in those areas so as to

ॐ

Gifts are a kind of visual aid that says, "I love you."

develop and build them up.

Another form of expression is **gift giving**. Many people need to see a tangible object that expresses love. Gifts are a kind of visual aid that says, "I love you." A gift demonstrates that you thought about them and your thought resulted in expending time and energy to get something to give to them.

Gifts don't have to be expensive. They can be things that you make or even things that you find. The monetary value is not the important thing. It is the fact that you took some time to think about it that makes the gift valuable. It is a token reflecting your thought for your mate. It is the thought behind the gift that is expressed by the gift. Impromptu gift giving can create memorable and special moments. Whatever time and money you do spend is a valuable investment in the quality of your marriage.

You may not be a gift giver by nature but it is easy to learn. Listen to your mate and hear what things are important to him or her. Take your spouse shopping and listen to the things that he or she likes and would love to buy. Learn how your mate thinks. If your mate receives love through gifts then it is well worth your time to learn how to give them.

A third kind of expression is through **physical touch**. If your mate receives love through this love language, he or she wants you to sit close, to hold hands, to hug and kiss. A back rub means a great deal to such a person. Touch does not have to be sexual, though sex is an important part of it. But this love language does require that you be close to your mate. You may not think of yourself as a touchy feely kind of person but if the primary way that your mate receives love is through touch you need to get over your reservations and learn to be close.

A fourth type of expression is **acts of service**. It means more than just waiting on someone. People who respond to this expression of love need their mate to do things for them and with them. They are very activity oriented. They can't sit down until everything is in order. They are high energy people, motivated by task. You mention a task and they're gone, trying to do it. They never procrastinate. They love to do things and they most feel loved when you do things with them. They are hobby people. They like sports.

If your spouse receives love through acts of service, the way to express love is to find out his or her list of chores for the day and offer to take some of them. Those are the things that are most important to them and by helping, you are placing yourself in their world. They love it when you do things and go places with them. They feel loved when you do things for them.

Some people need to have your full attention in order to feel loved.

These acts require time, effort and energy because you have to do something. You have to plan. These are not people who want to sit and chat. They have to be moving.

Quality time is the fifth form of expression. Some people need to have your full attention in order to feel loved.

They require undivided and undistracted focus from you. In the Song of Solomon we saw this in the form of going away to the country. If this is the love language of your mate, you need to plan time to get away on a regular basis, where you will not be interrupted. You need to listen to each other, even if your mate tells you the whole story ten times. Learn not to interrupt them. Connect to them emotionally as they are sharing. It is important to focus on them when they are speaking. Look into their eyes. Listen for their feelings. Observe their body language and give them praise.

Quality time has to be a healthy sharing. It is not a time to dump problems on your spouse. Rather it is a time for communicating dreams, desires, visions, plans and goals. It is a time for sharing feelings. Above all it is time for fun and laughter. People who receive love through quality time want to be a part of their mate's world and they want their mate to be a part of their world.

We have already seen that the marriage is a picture of the relationship between Jesus and the church. The ways that love is given and received are exactly according to the Word of God. The practical application is obvious but there is a direct parallel in God's love for us and in His expectation of love from us. We saw each form of expression in the Song of Solomon but the principles run through the entire Bible.

Most importantly, all five love languages are about setting our own wants and needs aside in order to concentrate on the wants and needs of the other. As with every aspect of marriage, it's not about you.

That is the way that God communicates with us and He expects us to be like Him when we communicate with each other. In fact every one of the five shows up in His expressions of His love to us.

The Bible itself is God's words of encouragement to us. In it we find a multitude of promises and declarations that let us know just what He thinks of us. He constantly reminds us that He loves us, that we are the apple of His eye, that we are more than conquerors in Him, that we have abundant life in Him.

Every part of His Word, when understood properly, is an encouragement to us to live to our fullest potential. We always know that God believes in us because He keeps telling us so.

Since God talks to us He wants us to treat Him the same. He wants us to pray, study His Word and learn about Him. He wants conversation and time alone with us.

God gives gifts in a variety of forms. Most prominent are the gifts of the Spirit. Everything we could ever need to live a life of victory is available from the Holy Spirit. In addition we have the fruits of the Spirit. God is daily giving us the gifts of peace, joy, faithfulness and righteousness, just to name a few. Every time we experience one of these gifts we are reassured that God loves us and wants good for us.

In return God asks us to give to Him. What we call tithes and offerings are, above all else, gifts that demonstrate our love and our appreciation to Him. They help to build His kingdom and that makes God very happy.

The presence of God is analogous to touch and physical closeness. In intimacy with Him we can actually feel His presence. He delights in expressing Himself to us through the anointing of the Holy Spirit. In return God desires us to seek His anointing so that we are close to Him. He exhorts us to draw near to Him so that He can draw near to us.

The working of His Word is his act of service to us. In fact Jesus is the Word. From the beginning He has served us, even to the point of laying down His life for us. Even now He stands at the right hand of the Father interceding for us. And His Word never stops working to bring us blessing, health and abundance.

We always know that God believes in us because he keeps telling us so.

God's desire is for us to act the same way. He desires that we lay our lives down to serve one another, to care for and have compassion for others.

As a fifth form of expression God desires to spend time with us. He is always available to share in our dreams, desires and hopes. He listens to them when we share them with Him and He constantly encourages us in the attainment of our destiny.

Likewise He wants us to share in His goals and His dreams. Above all he desires that all men be saved, and every time that we participate in sharing the love of God with others we are encouraging the fulfillment of God's dreams.

This analysis may seem over-simplified but the bottom line is that God has chosen to express love to us in the way that we can best receive it. He speaks to us in the language or mode of expression that we can understand. If you would learn this principle of communication in your marriage you would experience a tremendous increase in intimacy with your mate. Love means learning how your spouse receives love and adapting your expression of love to fit that language.

*Before critisizing
your wife's faults,
you must remember
that it may have
been those very
defects that
prevented her from
getting a better
husband.*

———————————

4

FASTER HORSES, YOUNGER WOMEN AND MORE MONEY THE PRACTICAL SIDE OF LOVE

Who is this coming out of the wilderness
Like pillars of smoke,
Perfumed with myrrh and frankincense,
With all the merchant's fragrant pow-
* ders?*
Behold, it is Solomon's couch,
With sixty valiant men around it,
Of the valiant of Israel.
They all hold swords,
Being expert in war.
Every man has his sword on his thigh
Because of fear in the night.
Of the wood of Lebanon
Solomon the King
Made himself a palanquin:
He made its pillars of silver,
Its support of gold,
Its seat of purple,
Its interior paved with love
By the daughters of Jerusalem.
Go forth, O daughters of Zion,
And see King Solomon with the crown

With which his mother crowned him
On the day of his wedding,
The day of the gladness of his heart.
(Song of Solomon 3:6-11)

As we read through the Song of Solomon we are so caught up in the romance of the story that it is easy to overlook a simple, but important fact. The groom was wealthy.

He had flocks (2:16). He had vineyards. He was financially successful and secure. His companions also had flocks (1:7), which means that he hung around with others who were successful as well. His bride had jewelry made of gold (1:10-11). The romance of Solomon was undergirded with money and financial security. This marriage had plenty.

The groom was Solomon. He was perfumed with myrrh and frankincense, both of which were more valuable than gold in the ancient world. He could afford to have sixty men following him around. He owned a palanquin, the translation of a word in Hebrew that literally means "couch." It was a kind of litter or chair that could be carried by several servants. It was made of gold, silver and expensive purple cloth. Solomon was rich.

He was the king so we might expect him to be rich, but a study of Solomon's life will demonstrate that he became rich because he sought wisdom, not because he was king. We can also see that being romantic is a lot easier when you can afford to go to nice restaurants, buy nice gifts and travel to exotic vacation spots.

Of course money is not a prerequisite to romance, and if you don't have much money you can still have a successful marriage. But that's not the point. It is still true that the single biggest factor contributing to divorce is the strain of financial problems. Struggling to pay bills and take care of everyday living can create tremendous tension between husband and wife. Most arguments can be traced back to some problem with money.

It is with this in mind that we need to discuss financial responsibility in a marriage. It is a vitally important part of the success of a relationship.

Being romantic is a lot easier when you can afford to go to nice restaurants, buy nice gifts and travel to exotic vacation spots.

We have a financial plan that we have used since before we were married. It is not complicated. Anyone can use it and if you do, you will know exactly where you stand financially every single day of the month. It will let you know without question if you can spend money or if you can't. You will know every minute, without worry or concern, if you will be able to pay your bills at the end of the month and, if you can't, what you will need to do in order to be able to.

What happens to most people is that they wait until the end of the month to find out where they are and by then, if they are behind, it is too late to remedy the situation.

Most Christians fail to set goals or make plans for their

finances. In fact, in every area of life they tend to let life dictate what's going to happen tomorrow. But the best way to change tomorrow is to create it. You need to plan goals and develop the self-discipline to carry them out.

You need goals for the week, the month, the next year, five years and ten years. Ask yourself where you want to be five years from now. If you don't have a plan then you won't get there. There will always

The best way to change tomorrow is to create it.

be something that eats away at your finances and five or ten years from now you will be in the same place you are now.

The husband is the responsible party in the marriage. That means that he is responsible for making sure there is enough money in the checking account to pay the bills. That doesn't mean the wife doesn't work. Today's society almost dictates that both will have to work. The wife might take care of the checkbook. If she is better at adding and subtracting, then it might be a good idea. It doesn't matter who takes care of the checkbook as long as the husband realizes he is responsible for making sure the money is there.

The plan we are presenting here will help in shouldering that responsibility. It is not enough to just believe that God will drop money out of the sky for you. You need a plan in order to accomplish financial stability.

What most people do is pick up a bill when it comes in the mail. They get paid on Friday. They write out a check.

They put it in an envelope, drive to the Post Office, buy a stamp, stamp the envelope and drop it in the mailbox. Then the bills are done for the week.

Whatever money is left over is what they feel they can spend for the week. With that they buy groceries, clothes, go to a movie and eat out.

The problem comes the next week. Suppose you pay the electric bill this week. You have quite a bit of money left because the bill isn't that big. So you buy some new shoes and new clothes and get some things for the house and go out for an expensive dinner and a show. All the money for the week is spent.

The next week rolls around and now two bills come due, the mortgage payment and the car payment. You didn't plan to deal with both of them at the same time and your pay-check isn't big enough to cover it all so you have to hold on to them and save some of this week's check until next week when you can send off both of them at once.

But the next week the bills for the VISA and the Sears card come in and now you have to borrow from the third and fourth weeks to pay these.

Each time you get a bill you make a separate trip to the Post Office. By the end of the month you've spent ten hours just getting stamps and you're a week behind on your pay-ments. By the end of three months you're a month behind and wondering how you will ever catch up.

This financial plan will alleviate those problems. Step one is to stop the habit of making the payments as soon as you get the bill. Instead, set a date each month when you are going to pay all the bills. The 30th, the end of the month, is the best time. Hold all your bills until the 30th and pay them all at the same time. When you enter agreements for any kind of payment, request them to come due on the 30th.

At the end of the month sit down and write out all of the checks together, stamp them all and make one trip to the Post Office. Buy a whole roll of stamps at one time. You have saved several hours of your time and all the bills are paid on time.

The second step in the plan is to have two checking accounts and one savings account. One of the checking accounts is used only for paying the monthly bills. No other money comes out of that account. The second checkbook is for everyday expenses, though it is better to learn to handle cash instead. Another problem that people often have is keeping track of the checkbook.

If you don't have it then you don't spend it.

They write a check for everything, no matter how small the expense. At the end of the month they have thirty checks to reconcile. They didn't get some of them entered in the check register. They don't remember how much they actually spent and they finally give up trying to balance the checkbook and just hope the bank got it right.

Because they don't know how much is really available they never know how much they can spend. They go to the store and see a great bargain on a television. It is only seventeen dollars a month. Can they afford it? Well, they had twenty dollars left over last week. So they buy it and at the end of the month find out that they really don't have enough.

By setting up a checking account exclusively for bills you will know how much is actually available for such purchases, and if you don't have it then you don't spend it.

Step three is designed to make sure you have enough money in your account to pay the bills at the end of the month. To do that, you need to figure out how much your total monthly bills are.

Most people will have a similar list of regular expenses — tithes and offerings, a house payment, car payment, insurance, electricity, phone, water. Credit card payments should be included. When making this list use the amount for your highest month for utilities. The total of these bills is the amount that you need to have in your account at the end of the month to cover all of your expenses.

Now you can compute how much of each paycheck is necessary to handle that amount. If you get paid weekly then you have four checks each month. Divide your total monthly expenses by four and that is the amount from each check that has to go into the checking account. If you get paid every two weeks then you have two paychecks each month. Divide the total by two and that amount has to go toward bills. That money is not available for anything else. It is already spent. You cannot touch it.

Whatever is left over is how much you have for all of

your other expenses — food, gas, entertainment, clothes. There is never any question about how much you can spend each week. You always know.

If you don't have enough money left over to buy food then you know what you need to do. There are only two alternatives that will work. One is to reduce your bills so that you aren't paying as much. The other is to make more money by getting a raise or working a second job. Spend less or make more. Those are the only options.

At least by following this plan you will always know exactly how much you need to have. You might have to get a second job for a while, until you pay off some debts to get rid of the monthly payments. But if you add up how much time you waste in an average week you will probably be shocked. The average American watches 28 hours of television every week, not counting time spent on video games, movies and the Internet. That's plenty of time for a part time job.

> *Spend less or make more. Those are the only options.*

The next step is to consider how to allocate the remaining money. You should set up an automatic pay to your savings account, even if it is a small amount. If you put aside twenty-five dollars a week for your whole life, by the time you retired you would have over a million dollars in your savings. It accrues at an amazing rate.

You should begin placing ten percent of your income

in other investments that pay dividends, such as stocks, bonds, IRA's, mutual funds and 401(k)'s. These kinds of things will start to bring in a regular income and ultimately provide you with great financial freedom.

One question that should be considered is, "What is debt?" Many people have a misunderstanding of exactly what debt means. Debt is when you owe more on something than you can liquidate it for.

Stop buying liabilities and start buying assets.

If you have a debt on your house of a hundred thousand dollars but you could sell it for a hundred and twenty thousand you do not have a debt. You have a twenty-thousand-dollar asset. If you go to the store and buy a thousand dollar refrigerator on credit, drive it home and right back again, you have a debt. Even if you didn't unload it from the truck you could not sell it for more than three hundred dollars. It is not an asset but a liability.

Financial success is not complicated. It is as simple as learning to control your spending so that you stop buying liabilities and start buying assets. Following this financial plan is a great place to start. Do this for a year and you will start to discover other benefits. Because you make payments consistently on time you will start to be offered better loan rates. Do it even for as little as six months and you will be amazed at how your credit report improves. Being on time saves you money.

Having financial stability will remove much of the stress from your marriage. And, as we said earlier, it is a lot easier to be romantic when you have money to spend.

Personal Story: Tom

Do I worry about my bills? No, because I know exactly how much I have. Years ago I was off work for seven months. I was part of a shop that had about a hundred and ten people and went down to about twelve or thirteen.

I was laid off but I had this budget already in place. I've used it since college, well over thirty years, and I've never departed from it. So I knew every week exactly how much money I needed to make that week in order to pay my bills at the end of the month.

So I went out and did what I had to do. It didn't matter if I made three dollars an hour or ten dollars an hour. I did what I had to do to make the money I needed to deposit that week. That's all I had to do. We lived better when I was laid off. We had more money than we knew what to do with. We were tithing. We were doing everything we knew to do.

At the end of seven months I made more money than if I had worked a regular full-time job. The budget gave me security. I knew exactly where I needed to be and how much I needed to put away every single week. Whatever was left over let me know whether we could eat, buy gas, go to a movie or buy clothes.

Following is a worksheet to use. I challenge you to follow this budget plan. It works.

Budget Work sheet

Expense: Absolutes (Monthly Amount)
These amounts are what you have to pay each month, no matter what.

Tithe = .10 x Monthly Salary _____

Offering _____

House Payment or Rent _____

Automobile Payment _____

Auto Insurance _____

Electricity _____

Gas _____

Phone _____

Water _____

Credit Card (_____) _____

Credit Card (_____) _____

Credit Card (_____) _____

Total Expenses: _____

Divided by paychecks per month ÷ _____
= Amount deposited into
 checking from each
 pay period = _____

Income:

Monthly (Take Home) Salary: _____

Minus Total Expenses: - _____

= Money for food, gas,
clothing, recreation, etc.: _____

A bachelor is a rolling stone that gathers no boss.

5

𝕾

ARE YOU ALL EARS?
THE ART OF LISTENING

You who dwell in the gardens,
The companions listen for your voice —
Let me hear it!
(Song of Solomon 8:13)

More than once the Song of Solomon alludes to the importance of the voice. We simply cannot escape the fact that the spoken word is an essential part of any relationship. Conversation is vital for a healthy marriage. There are some techniques for this area of communication that can help facilitate our communication skills. Conversation involves both speaking and listening, and there are things we can do to enhance both areas.

A powerful method is simply repeating back to your mate what you think he or she said. One of the biggest problems in communication is differences in perception. You say one thing but your spouse hears something completely different. Your mate says something to you and you hear something else, not what he or she said. We hear out of **our** perception, not **their** perception.

For example, we might say, "I was driving down the road one day and I saw a blue cow." There are different ways you can perceive or hear that statement and respond to it. Some would think the cow was painted the color blue. Others would wonder why the cow was sad. Still others might simply wonder where you could see a cow in the middle of a city. Your perception changes how you hear someone speak and their perception changes how they hear you speak.

Too often a husband will say something that is intended one way but the wife hears something that she perceives as threatening or insulting or abusive. Or the wife says something that is innocent in intent but the husband hears some kind of insult or reproach.

> *Your perception changes how you hear someone speak.*

By repeating back what you thought you heard, you give your mate an opportunity to correct your perception. Instead of getting angry, you stop and ask, "Is this what you are saying?" Your mate can respond by explaining what he or she really meant. In a short time you will find much greater intimacy in communication.

A second method in conversation is to examine your goals. What are you expecting in your marriage? What dreams did God put in you? What desires are there? As you answer these questions, write them down. A marriage, just as much as an individual, should have goals. Husband and wife need to discuss their goals and work toward them together.

Your individual goals may not always agree. The husband may want to build a successful business. The wife's desire may be simply to have a family. Or it might be the opposite; she wants a business and he wants a family. Whatever the case, it is important to identify those goals so that you can support your spouse in his or her pursuit. As with every other part of marriage, it is not about you. It is about giving into the other person's life by knowing their desires, encouraging them, supporting them, praying for them and helping them to reach their goals.

A third method of communication is learning to praise your spouse. Everyone needs to be built up. Saturate your mate with praise. It will help build security in them, and the more secure they feel, the more intimate your communication will become.

Fourth, learn the art of making the other person hear what you are saying. Learn to share in a way that makes them interested in what you have to say.

The principles of story telling are useful in everyday conversation. We love stories that keep us on the edge of our seats, stories that build anticipation and curiosity. If your mate seems preoccupied and not listening, try being creative. If you are really excited about something, you want to share it. But if you just blurt it out when they are busy with something else, they might react with a lot less enthusiasm than you would like.

But what if you hint at it instead of telling them? Say, "Something exciting happened. I'll tell you about it later." Then you build anticipation. You catch their attention and the whole thing becomes so much more exciting.

A fifth method of communication is to use creative

emotional word pictures. Illustrate what you are feeling by describing it as a picture. The Bible is filled with such images that convey a message. The parables of Jesus are classic examples of how God communicates to us in pictures.

> *Again, the kingdom of heaven is like treasure hidden in a field, which a man found and hid, and for joy over it he goes and sells all that he has and buys that field.* (Matthew 13:44)

The Song of Solomon is one word picture after another. They leave no doubt about what the speaker is saying.

> *I have come to my garden, my sister, my spouse;*
> *I have gathered my myrrh with my spice;*
> *I have eaten my honeycomb with my honey;*
> *I have drunk my wine with my milk.*
> (Song of Solomon 5:1)

Personal Story: Maureen
    I experienced a time in my life when I felt great insecurity. Because I came from a real insecure background, it would grip my heart over the littlest things. And I didn't know what was going on. We were in

Jamaica ministering and we had things to do. Tom was involved with all these meetings and he had to have study and preparation time. And I was getting to a place that I needed some quality time.

So I kept dropping hints, but I didn't say it clearly. I really didn't realize what was happening. I had a lot of meetings, too. But I just wanted to tell Tom everything God was showing me. So I went to him and said, "Let's talk. I've got to tell you these exciting things."

Tom answered, "I can't listen right now. I've got too much going on."

When he said that, I felt abandonment and insecurity. Inside I felt so worthless and worn out. I felt like I just wanted to run away and hide.

But God gave me a word picture. He said, "What you feel inside right now is like you're in the middle of the ocean and you're drowning and yelling for help and nobody's hearing you. And that is insecurity."

I had felt that before in my marriage and it was always a place of panic. But with this word picture I was able to express it to Tom. Without attacking him I was able to say that I was empty and how his words affected me. Of course he was not aware that I was hurt until I told him. Right away we knew what it was and we prayed together and it was gone. And I've never had that again.

℘

The flip side of communicating is listening. Perhaps you have noticed that a significant part of the suggestions we have made about communicating involve speaking or acting in such a way that your spouse listens to you. It is just as important for you to listen to your spouse. The deepest need of the human heart is to be heard. Your spouse wants to be respected and valued for who he or she is. A person who does not believe you are listening will never feel understood or accepted. A person who does believe you are listening will open his or her heart to you.

We all want to be understood but first we must make it a priority to understand.

> *He who answers before listening —*
> *That is his folly and his shame.*
> (Proverbs 18:13 NIV)

James expresses the same idea.

> *So then, my beloved brethren, let ev-*
> *ery man be swift to hear, slow to speak,*
> *slow to wrath.* (James 1:19)

Listening is a skill. It can be learned and it can be improved by developing a variety of techniques. First of all, it will help to know what a bad listener is. There are several ways of listening that are not good for the relationship.

Competitive listeners are those who compare themselves with the one talking. Instead of listening they are focused on who is smarter, more emotionally healthy, who has suffered more or who is better. The husband comes home and he has had a bad day. He can't wait to talk about it because he wants his wife's sympathy. He wants her to connect to his feelings.

The deepest need of the human heart is to be heard.

Instead she says, "You think you had a bad day. Let me tell you what happened to me." Suddenly there is a competition over who has suffered the most.

It could go the other way around. The wife had a bad day and she can hardly wait to tell her husband about it but as soon as she does he counters it with his own experience. Either way it is bad listening.

A second form of bad listening is **mind reading.** Mind reading refers to listeners who try to analyze what you are really thinking and feeling instead of paying attention to what you are actually saying. Because of this they miss what you are trying to communicate and instead, focus on things you never meant and never said. The wife says, "I'm so tired tonight that I just want to put my feet up and read a book."

The husband, instead of listening to what she says, thinks to himself, "She's only saying that. What she really wants is to go to a movie." It is important in communication to believe that whatever a person says is what he really means.

The third bad listening trait is **rehearsing**. This means going over in your mind what you are going to say instead of listening to what the other person is saying. You say to yourself, "As soon as she pauses I'll say this and then she'll probably say this, so then I'll say this and then that."

You are too busy preparing your response to actually listen. You look interested but your mind is racing to the next point you want to make. It is bad listening because your attention is not on what your spouse is saying but on what you will say when your spouse is done.

Fourth is **filtering**. Filtering means that you only pay enough attention to see if the person is angry or unhappy or in emotional danger. It is an emotional moment and your spouse starts talking to you. Your immediate thought is, "Am I in trouble? Did I do something?" You listen to find out those answers and as soon as you are sure that you are safe, you stop listening and mentally go somewhere else. Your mind wanders off and you filter out every other bit of information.

Judging is a fifth type of poor listening. Judging means assuming ahead of time that the person speaking is stupid or unqualified and therefore not worth listening to. For example, your spouse starts telling you about a book that he or she read and instead of listening to what they are saying, you start to ask yourself what qualifies them to talk about this subject. "Who does he think he is? I'm smarter than him." Such listeners dismiss most of the conversation before it is even spoken. They don't listen at all.

Personal Story: Maureen

Tom reads constantly, learning everything he can. He's always in the middle of a book — about finances or health, or he is studying the Bible. He is very knowledgeable about many things. So I have to be careful that I don't think to myself, "Well, who gave him a PhD?" If I do that then I stop listening. I need to draw from the things that he is saying because he has read it and learned it. The truth is that I don't want to read about health. All I want to know is what I'm supposed to do. So you just tell me what I'm supposed to do and I'll do it.

Sixth is **dreaming**. Dreaming occurs when something that the person says triggers a chain of thoughts in your own mind. You remember something that is similar in your own experience and you drift off into that world and space out everything else that is said. You live in the emotions and the feelings of the remembered event so much that you are there — and not in the conversation where you should be listening. You are a dreamer and dreamers make poor listeners. They don't hear anything their spouse says.

A seventh type of poor listening that is similar to dreaming is **identifying** or **self-centered listening**. The person says something and it reminds you of something in your own life. Instead of listening you can't wait for them to finish so that you can relate your own experience. "Oh, I went through the same thing. Let me tell you about my experience." It is self-centered because you are pulling them out of their world and into yours. Good listening does not pull the attention away from the person speaking.

Advice listeners think of themselves as great problem solvers. After hearing a few sentences they focus on giving the right advice. They are more concerned, however, with problem solving than with deepening the relationship. They can't wait until you stop talking so that they can give you an answer. Most of the time, people don't really want advice when they share problems with friends or mates. They just want to talk it out, to express their frustration or anger or whatever emotion. If they want advice they will normally tell you that. Unsolicited advice is simply poor listening.

——— ℘ ———

Unsolicited advice is simply poor listening.

———

A ninth form of poor listening is **arguing**. Some people are more interested in arguing than in listening. They listen but their attention is focused on the opposite of what they are hearing because they are going to disagree as soon as you are done. They love to disagree. If you say it is red they will claim it is pink. Arguing is not really listening at all.

Related to arguing is the listener who is more concerned with **being right** than he is with listening. Such people can't take suggestions to change. You present something to them in the appropriate manner for resolving conflict and instead of working on the problem, they go to great lengths just to avoid being wrong.

They make all kinds of excuses. They twist facts, start shouting, make accusations and call up your past sins to deflect attention from themselves. Someone who thinks he is always right doesn't listen to what others say.

Derailing is a technique that changes the direction of the conversation. Derailing listeners quickly get bored or uncomfortable with what you are saying. As soon as you stop to take a breath they change the subject. They make a joke or a quip or bring up something completely unrelated in order to avoid seriously listening. You may not have been finished with what you were saying but you get derailed by the subject change.

A twelfth type of poor listening is **pretend listening**. A pretend listener doesn't hear a word you are saying. He makes all the right gestures and acts like he is really into the conversation, but ten minutes later he won't remember a thing you said because he was not really listening. He was just going through the motions.

Pretend listening happens frequently in marriage. And it is poor listening. There is a tendency for a husband and wife to get excited about things and start telling each other, but neither one is listening to the other. No one is hearing. They are talking to themselves. It is an example of poor listening. Of course, there are some who don't even pretend. They just don't listen at all. That's even worse.

What all of these bad listening traits have in common is a self-centered motivation. Instead of listening, people do whatever they can to turn the conversation to themselves. If any of them describe you, you need to take steps to change.

What is a good listener? By contrast to poor listening it is "others" oriented. To be a good listener you must learn to listen to the heart of the person, the innermost expression of his or her thoughts, desires and dreams. You must listen to understand the person. Listen with your eyes, heart and ears.

Good listening starts with your motivation. When you are listening to your spouse with the right motive you have four intentions. You want to understand them. You want to enjoy your mate. You want to learn something from him or her and you want to help. You listen with a heart of mercy. You try to see the world as your mate sees it. You don't try to win the conversation because when you approach conversation in a competitive way, whether you win or lose, you will lose the relationship.

> *What all of these bad listening traits have in common is a self-centered motivation.*

A good listener is an active listener. To become active means to take steps that will assure your spouse that you are listening and encouraging him or her to share and to speak. You can begin by learning to paraphrase. As you are listening, begin to tell the story to yourself, asking yourself what your spouse is saying and what he or she means. You relive it in your own words so that you have it in your mind in a way that you can understand it.

It is important to let your mate finish. Most people can't be quiet for more than fifteen seconds before they feel compelled to interupt. But that is poor listening. Repeat the information back in your own warm, caring words. Now you've stepped into their world. You've taken an interest in where they are living.

Most people can't be quiet for more than fifteen seconds before they feel compelled to interupt.

Next, clarify the story by asking reflective questions. "Is this what you are saying? Is this what you meant?" By asking these questions you will get even more of the picture. This gives your mate an opportunity to address any misunderstandings that might arise from the conversation. He or she can tell you if you are getting a wrong perception and correct it before it causes problems.

Once you have understood what your mate is saying you can move to the next question. "How do you feel?" By encouraging your mate to express the feeling of the situation you are establishing a connection in the area of the soul that is extremely important to the marriage. When a person shares feelings, automatically the heart opens and the inner person is able to come out. Above all, that person feels important, valued and loved because you took the time to listen, understand and care.

The most important part of listening is reaching out to your mate's need. It is only when the heart opens and feelings are expressed that you can really ask what the need is and identify it. You may find that the only need your spouse had at that point was to express the feelings that he or she was experiencing. Just the act of talking it out will often settle the whole matter. Once the truth is out in the open the enemy can't play it any more.

Only after listening in this way should you begin to offer feedback. Your objective is to look for your mate's feelings. In a non-judgmental way, share your reactions. Make it clear that you want to understand his or her perspective. It is only after going through all of the steps of good listening that you should ask, "Do you want any advice?" and you should be prepared to keep quiet if they tell you that they don't. They may not be ready to confront the situation and resolve it yet. Recognize that it's more important to the relationship that you listened than that you gave advice.

Good listening involves your motivation, your attitude and even your body language. It is important to keep eye contact. Lean forward slightly while you are listening. Encourage your spouse to talk by nodding your head. Ask questions that help clarify what is being said.

Actively move away from distractions. Women are especially impressed when their husbands turn off the television in order to talk to them. Anything that takes your attention away from your spouse is detrimental to the relationship.

To be a good listener you must be committed to the principles that we have discussed in this chapter. You need to be determined to understand your spouse so much that you will not give up on it. It may be that you won't like what you hear. Sometimes when people become completely honest, especially if they are expressing feelings, the words that come out are not pretty. Decide now that you will not react defensively but you will seek to understand. If you need to change something that you have been doing, then change it. If you need to fast and pray for a few days then do it. Praying together is one of the best ways to build intimate conversation.

But first listen and understand. Paraphrase what your spouse says. Repeat it back to him or her. Ask questions to clarify anything you don't understand. Ask how your spouse feels and ask what the need is. It's even a good idea to take notes. Write it out.

These steps in listening are proactive. They require that you take the initiative. Don't wait for your spouse to do it. By following these methods you put yourself in the right position and attitude to be a good listener. You have gone right to the heart and created an intimate connection. Once his or her heart is open and your spouse knows that you have tried to understand, then you will be able to give advice. But you have to wait until the heart is open and they feel like you care about them as a person. The end result is a healthier and stronger marriage.

*It's easy for a
married couple
to acquire
mutual interests.
All he has to do is
what she likes.*

6

YOU TALK TOO MUCH
LEARNING TO COMMUNICATE

He brought me to the banqueting house,
And his banner over me was love.
Sustain me with cakes of raisins,
Refresh me with apples,
For I am lovesick.
His left hand is under my head;
And his right hand embraces me.
I charge you, O daughters of Jerusalem,
By the gazelles or by the does of the field,
Do not stir up nor awaken love
Until it pleases.

(Song of Solomon 2:4-7)

The emotions of love can be overwhelming. The bride in Song of Solomon makes several statements through the course of the poem that indicate how much she is affected. For example, in 2:5 she says she is "lovesick," a phrase that is repeated in 5:8.

The Hebrew word indicates that she was "faint" from the effects of love. In chapter 2 it could be that she is worn out or exhausted from love. In chapter 5 she is not with her lover, meaning that she is faint from his absence.

The implication from the text, if we express it in nonpoetic language, is that his absence results in her basic needs not being met and she is left in a weakened condition as a result.

In 2:7 the bride gives a warning. "Do not stir up nor awaken love until it pleases." It is an odd phrase that is difficult to translate. In essence it is a warning not to leap into the emotions of love until you are ready for them. If you are not prepared, love will take a physical and emotional toll. Love is not for the weak.

Many comments could be made about this passage but a couple of things are particularly important. There are specific needs that the bride has, especially emotional needs, and if they are not met it has a direct impact on her well-being.

Secondly, she communicates those needs to her mate. We will find that honest communication is a necessary part of successful marriage.

The groom has needs also, needs met only in the bride. It is interesting how she describes her impact on him.

> *I am a wall,*
> *And my breasts like towers;*
> *Then I became in his eyes*
> *As one who found peace.*
>
> (Song of Solomon 8:10)

The first two lines refer in a poetic style to sexual intimacy. The last two lines indicate that through her union with him she brought him peace.

The New International Version makes it even clearer.

I am a wall,
and my breasts are like towers.
Thus I have become in his eyes
like one bringing contentment.
(Song of Solomon 8:10 NIV)

Love is a decision. It is not about you. It is about the other person. This attitude of giving, of selflessness, is essential if a marriage is to be healthy.

But this doesn't mean that personal needs stop. We all have them and when they are not met it becomes very difficult to meet the needs of others. It is hard to give anything when you are empty.

The emotional, physical and spiritual needs that we have should be met in a marriage but we must never allow our needs to be the reason we are in the relationship. A healthy marriage is the one in which we seek to meet the needs of our mate. We have needs that must be met and we must meet the needs of our mate. A balance is necessary.

It is much easier to meet the needs of your mate if you understand what they are. We all have some very basic things that are necessary for healthy life.

First is the need for unconditional love. We talked about it in an earlier chapter. It is the kind of love that is a decision. I decide to love you without any kind of qualifications. It is not based on emotion or whim or chemistry.

Unconditional love says, "I will always love you. You don't have to perform. You don't have to earn it." Unconditional love does not keep a record of wrong. It forgives and it forgets. It is not sensitive and does not take offense. It is not touchy.

Everyone needs to be loved without conditions attached.

We recognize that in marriage, unconditional love is the kind of love we must give. It is important to understand that it is also the type of love that we need to be given. People who are not given assurance that they are loved just because they exist, spend much of their time trying to perform. They are always afraid that if they don't act just right then love will be withheld from them. It is extremely difficult for them to ever give much into the relationship because they are so concerned about their own position. Everyone needs to be loved without conditions attached.

The second basic need is to be appreciated. When people believe that no one notices their efforts they stop making any effort at all. A few words of acknowledgment can go a long way toward building your mate's self confidence and esteem. In our marriage we made a commitment to each other that every time we did something for each other, no matter how small it might be, we would stop and say, "Thank you." By doing this you will never begin to take your mate for granted. And one of your mate's most basic needs will be met.

A third need is for security. Every person needs to feel secure. This is something we should be doing every day. My spouse needs to know that in my mind this is forever. I'm not going to leave if I don't get my way. I'm not threatening divorce. I'm not packing my bags. I'm not going home to mother. I'm not going anywhere. We're in this forever and we will work out whatever we need to work out.

When that sense of security is lacking, people are much less likely to work out problems. They will run rather than talk or they will not express their own needs out of fear that their mate will run or react negatively. When insecurity enters the marriage it is very hard to get rid of and a basic need is left unfulfilled. A marriage needs security to be healthy.

Every wife should become her husband's greatest cheerleader and every husband should become his wife's biggest fan.

The fourth need is for purpose. All people need to believe that there is a reason for their life, that they have goals, that they have been put on this earth with a destiny. Without purpose we become aimless and the result is depression and frustration. It is in the marriage that destiny most needs to be spoken. Your mate needs to know that he or she has value.

The fifth need is for confidence. To function effectively in life we must know that we can do whatever we need to do to accomplish our destiny.

Lack of confidence affects every area of a relationship. It can lessen the respect you have for your spouse. "I'm a loser and you chose to marry me, so you must be a loser, too." It doesn't take long before this attitude will undermine the whole foundation of the marriage. Every wife should become her husband's greatest cheerleader and every husband should become his wife's biggest fan.

Every person has these needs and if they are not met then the marriage suffers. Unfortunately, too many couples fail to understand the dynamics of this part of the relationship. They tend to go one direction or the other. Some devote themselves to meeting the needs of their spouse without any regard to their own needs. In a very short time they have nothing left to give.

Others spend all their time trying to coerce or manipulate their spouse into meeting their needs. The result is a mate who is drained and resentful.

The answer, of course, lies between these two extremes. Our focus should be on meeting the needs of our mate but when we feel a lack in our own needs we have to find ways to communicate that lack to our mate without manipulation or coercion. This is a major part of the art of communication.

The sharing of needs is the highest form of communication. As such it is the most dangerous and the most difficult, but in marriage it is also the most important.

We all learn to communicate at different levels. The first is superficial communication. It is limited to very shallow comments that really don't mean anything. "How are you today?" You don't usually care how they are, but you had to say something in order to be nice or at least to avoid being rude. In fact, if the person responded by giving you a detailed analysis of his condition you would feel that you were being imposed on and your time wasted. You would not only not care, but you would expect the person to understand that you don't care and just answer with the same shallowness you addressed them with: "I'm fine."

Superficial conversation does little more than acknowledge the other person's presence. It is very safe since it requires no commitment and no vulnerability on your part. A marriage that has only superficial communication will never be much of a marriage.

The second level of communication is the sharing of facts. "Did you hear about that accident this morning?" "I hear that Congress raised taxes." "It was 105 degrees today."

Sharing facts is much like getting or giving a news report. It is nothing but an exchange of information. It is also very safe. You give facts but you don't give yourself.

Sharing facts is a good place for a couple to start communicating, especially when the facts they share concern each other. Wives love to know what their husbands did all day and to share with them what they did themselves. It is an important part of communication but it is only a starting place for more intimate conversation.

The third level of communication is not as safe as the first two. It happens when you begin to share your opinion.

You begin to express how you personally feel about something. It is not safe because if the other person does not agree with you it could lead to an argument.

In a healthy marriage both husband and wife encourage each other to think for themselves and to express what is on their hearts and minds. They don't always agree but they don't put each other down for their opinions, either. They don't call each other "dumb" or "stupid" or "weird" or anything else. If you are threatened by your mate's disagreement then there is some area of insecurity in you that needs to be worked on.

> *In a healthy marriage both husband and wife encourage each other to think for themselves.*

Couples must learn to disagree agreeably. There is an old saying in business that whenever two partners agree on everything, one of them isn't necessary. The fact that husband and wife don't always agree adds depth to the relationship. Being one does not mean thinking exactly alike. The freedom for husband and wife to each have their own opinions is vital in healthy communication.

With the fourth level of communication you start to develop real intimacy. Level four is expressing feelings or emotions. This requires a certain level of trust since the feelings are even more a part of you than opinions are. To share a feeling is to expose your inner personality. It makes you vulnerable. Negative feelings tend to elicit negative responses so it can be dangerous. Intimacy in a relationship, however, requires this level of sharing. A wrong way to share negative feelings is to call your best friend or friends to tell them what your spouse did.

In fact, it is really best to deal with negative feelings before they become a problem. Feelings come from thoughts. If you learn to control your thoughts then negative feelings will no longer be a problem. As you die to them they will die to you. Think positive. Focus on that which is good. Good thoughts will create healthy emotions.

> *Finally, brethren, whatever things are true, whatever things are noble, whatever things are just, whatever things are pure, whatever things are lovely, whatever things are of good report, if there is any virtue and if there is anything praiseworthy—meditate on these things.* (Philippians 4:8)

The highest level of communication is when you begin to share needs. It is the most dangerous level because you become the most vulnerable. Consequently it requires the greatest level of trust. But it is also the most important. A marriage is at its healthiest when husband and wife feel freedom to share their deepest needs, desires and feelings. With this kind of communication the husband has complete confidence that his wife will not deride him but rather try to meet his needs, and the wife has full confidence that her husband will not despise or judge her but will try to meet her needs. Sharing needs is an integral part of real love. Without sharing it is too easy for needs to go unnoticed.

In the Garden of Eden, before sin, Adam and Eve had complete openness.

> *And they were both naked, the man and his wife, and were not ashamed.* (Genesis 2:25)

The ideal state of being for a husband and wife is when there is nothing between them that causes shame. Good communication coupled with godly love that does not judge will produce a healthy marriage, utterly without either shame or arrogance of any kind. The highest level of intimacy occurs when the marriage is healthy and has intimacy in the soul area.

> *The ideal state of being for a husband and wife is when there is nothing between them that causes shame.*

Love, honor and respect must always regulate the fourth and fifth levels of communication. Respect, which is derived from the Latin word *respicere*, literally means to look at a person as he or she is without trying to change them. Respect is listening to your mate's deepest thoughts, feelings and needs without judgment.

*Marriage is
made in heaven.
So is thunder
and lightning.*

7

ℬ
IF YOU'RE GREEN, YOU'RE GROWING
LEARNING TO CHANGE

Let him kiss me with the kisses of his
mouth—
For your love is better than wine.
Because of the fragrance of your good
ointments,
Your name is ointment poured forth;
Therefore the virgins love you.
Draw me away!
(Song of Solomon 1:2-4)

In the New Testament there are two words used for love. *Philos* is an emotional, passionate kind of love. *Agape* is a more reasoned love, a decision rather than a feeling. *Philos* is not a bad thing. In fact a marriage that has no passion is pretty boring. It needs to be present in a relationship. It should not be the foundation of the marriage, however. It is just too unstable. Romance usually starts with passion but it needs to grow into *agape* love if it is to last. True love grows over time as it changes and becomes more and more mature.

Love is not static. It is always growing into greater and greater maturity. In the Song of Solomon we can see four different levels of love. They move from passion to purpose, from emotion to commitment.

The first is honeymoon love. It is the fun part of love. On your honeymoon you didn't care about anything but your mate. You didn't care if the bills got paid. You didn't care what the rest of the world was doing. You had romance. The only thing that mattered was the two of you. You got away and had a good time together.

The bride in the Song of Solomon has this in mind when she speaks of their love. "Draw me away." In the next verse she says, "The King has brought me into his chambers." They are caught up in the romantic passion of honeymoon love.

This kind of love should never leave a marriage. It needs to be planned so that it always has room for expression. A date night is important so that at least one night a week you are focused on each other without any other cares, a night of fun, laughter and light heartedness. Cares and circumstances and problems are not allowed on that night. Problems of the day are set aside and nothing is allowed to interfere.

Love is not static. It is always growing.

We have had a date night since we were newly married. Our kids were raised with the understanding that mom and dad have a night that they spend alone. Even when we didn't have a lot of money we found ways to make it work. There are inexpensive things you can do that are romantic and passionate. You can have a picnic at the park. You can go to the lake. We used to go to a nice restaurant and order one dinner with two plates. We would tell them we weren't very hungry. That way the evening wasn't too expensive. The romance was more important than the food.

Once a year you need to get away for a special time together, a yearly honeymoon, during which you focus on your mate. You speak the language of a honeymoon. What is this language? Psalm 45 is a wedding song. It expresses the passion of honeymoon love.

> *My heart is overflowing with a good theme;*
> *I recite my composition concerning the King;*
> *My tongue is the pen of a ready writer.*
> (Psalm 45:1)

The bride's heart is stirred. There is passion. What she sings comes from her heart, from who she is and from the depths of what he means to her. Another translation says, "My heart boils over with goodly words." Still another says, "My heart is overflowing with beautiful thoughts." What is in her heart just comes out.

> *For out of the abundance of the heart*
> *his mouth speaks.* (Luke 6:45)

The bride's tongue becomes a ready or skillful writer because what is in her heart comes out of her mouth. What she says will be written on his heart as well. Having good

thoughts about your mate is important for honeymoon love.
She goes on to speak positive words over her husband.

You are fairer than the sons of men;
Grace is poured upon your lips;
Therefore God has blessed you forever.
(Psalm 45:2)

She is saying, "You have a tremendous personality. I
see God's call on you. You have a destiny. You are anointed
of God and I see God's blessing and favor on you." Another
translation says, "Charm flows through your lips." She feels
that he always knows just what to say. Throughout this song
the message of the bride is that she prizes every moment they
spend together.

The language of honeymoon love is not one-sided either. The groom has his turn in the conversation.

You have ravished my heart,
My sister, my spouse;
You have ravished my heart
With one look of your eyes,
With one link of your necklace.
How fair is your love,
My sister, my spouse!
How much better than wine is your love,
And the scent of your perfumes
Than all spices!

Your lips, O my spouse,
Drip as the honeycomb;
Honey and milk are under your tongue;
And the fragrance of your garments
Is like the fragrance of Lebanon.
(Song of Solomon 4:9-11)

What is the groom saying? If we put it in less poetic terms he is speaking positive thoughts. "You come first in my life. I'm glad I am married to you. You are my best friend. If I had it to do all over again I would still marry you. As always you look terrific. I trust you. You make me feel good and I can't imagine life without you." He praises her beauty, her dress and her jewelry. He calls her blessed.

Honeymoon love is fun. It results from a decision to have romance and a determination to plan time for it. It is vital to a healthy marriage but it is only the beginning.

The second kind of love in the Song of Solomon is a negative type. It is immature love. We find the groom calling for his bride to join him.

My beloved spoke, and said to me:
"Rise up, my love, my fair one,
And come away.
For lo, the winter is past,
The rain is over and gone.
The flowers appear on the earth;
The time of singing has come,

And the voice of the turtledove
Is heard in our land.
The fig tree puts forth her green figs,
And the vines with the tender grapes
Give a good smell.
Rise up, my love, my fair one,
And come away!
O my dove, in the clefts of the rock,
In the secret places of the cliff,
Let me see your face.
Let me hear your voice;
For your voice is sweet,
And your face is lovely."
(Song of Solomon 2:10-14)

The groom summons his bride to leave the house and join him outdoors. He speaks of the vineyard, of spring, of the blossoming of the flowers and trees. He is a farmer, a gardener, and he calls for her to be part of his life, to see what he is doing, what his dreams are.

But the honeymoon is over and she apparently has no interest in his dreams anymore. The reference to the cliffs indicates that she has made herself inaccessible. The Hebrew word for "rock," *sela'* in the first line of verse 14, is a common word for large rocks.

The bride is located in the clefts of the rock, that is, she has hidden herself. The word translated "cliffs," *madrega*, is very rare in the Bible. It usually refers to the cliffs of Edom, such as the area around Petra, with very narrow passages and caves. She hides in the "secret places of the cliff." The bride conceals herself from her mate, just when he asks her to be interested in his activities. The next verse further indicates a problem.

> *Catch us the foxes,*
> *The little foxes that spoil the vines,*
> *For our vines have tender grapes.*
> (Song of Solomon 2:15)

The picture is of foxes loose in the vineyard, destroying the fruit. The implication is that her indifference is threatening the blossoming relationship. Her love has left the fun honeymoon state and become immature. Immature love is very destructive and can seriously damage a marriage. If you're not interested in your mate's interests, dreams, jobs and hobbies then you have a love that takes rather than gives. You are wrapped around yourself and stuck at a child's two-year-old level. The two-year-old syndrome is a focus on self. The world revolves around "me." It is "I, I, I" and "me, me, me." It is a selfish kind of love that cannot submit to giving.

The person who lives in immature love is a spoiled brat.

People who marry out of immature love marry for what their spouse can do for them. They don't want to hear anything about the other person's dreams or goals. Such love will not build a kingdom marriage.

The person who lives in immature love is a spoiled brat. Mature love doesn't mean spoiled. It is never manipulative. It is not driven by fear or by the law. It does not seek to control.

The next stage of love is just the opposite of an immature, taking love. It is a mature giving love. As the Song of Solomon progresses we find that the bride changes. It becomes her idea to go to the country. She has taken an interest in his life.

I am my beloved's,
And his desire is toward me.
Come, my beloved,
Let us go forth to the field;
Let us lodge in the villages.
Let us get up early to the vineyards;
Let us see if the vine has budded,
Whether the grape blossoms are open,
And the pomegranates are in bloom.
There I will give you my love.
The mandrakes give off a fragrance,
And at our gates are pleasant fruits,
All manner, new and old,
Which I have laid up for you, my beloved.
(Song of Solomon 7:10-13)

With mature love you enter the world of your spouse. You take an active interest in his or her dreams and desires. You submit your will to what makes the other person happy. You discover and enjoy your mate's gifts and talents. You get involved in their hobbies and activities. You learn to enjoy what they enjoy. Mature love is about giving.

Personal Story: Maureen

I was a bookworm. I liked to sit and read books and I didn't like to do any kind of sports at all. But my husband enjoys many outdoor activities. So what did I have to do? I had to learn to ski. I had to learn to golf. I had to learn to enjoy bike riding. I had to take up hiking. And today I love those things.

Tom goes shopping with me. Now he doesn't like it when I buy things without him. He wants to help pick out my clothes.

From mature love comes responsible love. We see the groom portrayed in a role of responsibility. We have already seen that he worked. He was a farmer, a gardener. He was also a protector of the family.

Who is this coming out of the wilderness
Like pillars of smoke,

> *Perfumed with myrrh and frankincense,*
> *With all the merchant's fragrant pow-*
> *ders?*
> *Behold, it is Solomon's couch,*
> *With sixty valiant men around it,*
> *Of the valiant of Israel.*
> *They all hold swords,*
> *Being expert in war.*
> *Every man has his sword on his thigh*
> *Because of the fear in the night.*
>   (Song of Solomon 3:6-8)

Responsible love means taking on responsibility for the family. It is very important that the husband be the provider and the protector. But this does not mean the wife doesn't work. Proverbs 31 makes it clear that a godly wife carries a certain responsibility as well. Both husband and wife need a caring and serving attitude.

The highest level of love is called transforming love. It implies a willingness to change. We see an incident that begins with a selfish attitude from the bride that prompts a similar reaction from the groom, who then leaves. Ultimately she becomes willing to change and goes in search of him to put the situation right.

> *I sleep, but my heart is awake;*
> *It is the voice of my beloved!*
> *He knocks, saying,*

"Open for me, my sister, my love,
My dove, my perfect one;
For my head is covered with dew,
My locks with the drops of the night."
I have taken off my robe;
How can I put it on again?
I have washed my feet;
How can I defile them?
My beloved put his hand
By the latch of the door,
And my heart yearned for him.
I arose to open for my beloved,
And my hands dripped with myrrh,
My fingers with liquid myrrh,
On the handles of the lock.
I opened for my beloved,
But my beloved had turned away and was
   gone.
My heart leaped up when he spoke.
I sought him, but I could not find him;
I called him, but he gave me no answer.
(Song of Solomon 5:2-6)

Many changing emotions are expressed in this passage.
There is offense, anger and insecurity. But there is also repentance and death to self. Myrrh is an interesting symbol in
this context. It was a very valuable type of incense in the
ancient world. Not only did it have a fragrant scent but it was

used in a wide variety of applications.

It was a chemical used for embalming, from which we can associate it in this passage of scripture with death to self. But it was also widely used as a medicine, treating such problems as cancer, leprosy, syphilis and herpes. It was used as an anti-infectious, anti-inflammatory, antiseptic, astringent and as a tonic. It symbolized healing and preservation.

> *If love is not constantly growing, changing and maturing, then it is not love.*
>
> *True love grows.*

In the context of the Song of Solomon myrrh pictures a death to self that results in repentance, a change of attitude, healing and the preservation of the relationship. Unwillingness to change is destructive to a marriage. We all need to allow the Holy Spirit to show us those areas where we need to die to self, those things that we must let go. Ultimately if love is not constantly growing, changing and maturing, then it is not love. True love grows.

The mate you got
is the one you
caught with the
bait you got.

8

TO LOVE OR TO LEAVE
LOVE AS A DECISION

I am dark, but lovely,
O daughters of Jerusalem,
Like the tents of Kedar,
Like the curtains of Solomon.
Do not look upon me, because I am
    dark,
Because the sun has tanned me.
My mother's sons were angry with me;
They made me the keeper of the vine-
    yards,
But my own vineyard I have not kept.
                    (Song of Solomon 1:5-6)

Love feels great. That's why we love it. But because it is an emotion it is dreadfully unstable. It can change from ecstasy to pain in a hurry. The insecurity that is so often a part of romantic experience comes from this instability.

Early in the Song of Solomon the bride expresses some of this doubt about herself. It begins with a concern for her appearance. She is dark because the sun has burned her, that is, because she has been tanned.

Today a tan is considered beautiful, but this was not always the case. How it is regarded depends on the perceptions of the culture. In modern society people of the lower working class spend most of their time indoors, working in offices or factories. It is the upper class, the affluent, who have time to lie in the sun and get tanned. Tans are beautiful because they are associated with affluence and success.

In the past, when the world was primarily agricultural, the lower class workers spent most of their time outdoors. Light skin indicated that you were so affluent that you didn't have to work in the fields. You could spend your time indoors instead, pursuing a life of leisure. Light, untanned skin used to be regarded as the most beautiful. Dark, tanned skin indicated a low place in society.

Love that lasts begins as a decision and then becomes a feeling.

The bride is dark because she has to work in the vineyards. In these verses she is defending her beauty. When she says "I am dark, *but* lovely," she is asserting that her beauty does not depend on social status. She expresses a concern that she will not be loved because of her low position.

She also implies that there were problems in her family. She became dark because she worked in the vineyards. And she worked in the vineyards because her brothers made her. And her brothers made her work because they were angry with her.

The bride is afraid that she will not be loved because she is dark, low class and has a family that holds her back.

This insecurity comes from the emotional side of love. It is just not stable enough to last. The bride began with this unstable and insecure foundation. Most of the pain of love stories can be traced to the emotions of love.

Fortunately the Bible gives us a godly view of what love can and should be. The groom in the Song of Solomon overlooks all of these problems that plague the bride's mind.

> *Behold, you are fair, my love!*
> *Behold, you are fair!*
> (Song of Solomon 1:15)

What makes this possible is the fact that the groom's love, while charged with intense emotion, is not based on emotion. He has decided to love her and that is that.

Love is a decision. It is the result of an act of will. That does not mean it is without feeling. The feelings of love are wonderful. But love that lasts begins as a decision and then becomes a feeling.

In the last chapter we alluded to the two words used in the New Testament for love. *Philos* is the kind of love most people mean when they speak of falling in love. It is often translated "brotherly love," but this is not exactly the right definition. It is more properly called "passionate love."

It is emotionally based. It is chemistry. It is dependent primarily on feelings. When we say we are "in love" it is this passion that we are talking about. The other kind of love, the kind used to describe God's love for us, is *agape*. It is the kind of love that Paul described in his letter to the Corinthians, the description read so often at weddings.

> *Love suffers long and is kind; love does not envy; love does not parade itself, is not puffed up; does not behave rudely, does not seek its own, is not provoked, thinks no evil; does not rejoice in iniquity, but rejoices in the truth; bears all things, believes all things, hopes all things, endures all things. Love never fails.* (1 Corinthians 13:4-8)

Agape love is not based on feeling. It is defined as an undefeatable act of kindness, an unquenchable good will that always seeks the highest good for the other person, no matter what they've done or not done. In short, it is a reasoned decision, not an emotion. It is a choice. Therefore, because it is a decision, it is not dependent on the mood of the moment. *Agape* love is not based on chemistry.

Emotions last as long as the circumstances sustain them. Love that is based on a decision lasts forever.

When we have this kind of love in a marriage it means that we start every day seeking the highest good for our mates. We wake up each morning with a decision that says, "I want the best for my mate this day, no matter what. I want this to happen regardless of what he's done. I want to put kindness and love in her life no matter what's going on.

Successful marriage is about being kind and being loving to each other. We have been married for thirty-six years. When we got married we felt a passion and love that seemed it would never die. Now, after more than three decades, our passion is greater than it was when we were dating.

But the reason passion has lasted is because we make a decision every morning that we will love. We choose daily to seek the highest good for each other. Emotions last as long as the circumstances sustain them. Love that is based on a decision lasts forever.

We are not saying that this kind of love is easy. But we have the love of God to draw from.

> *Now hope does not disappoint, because the love of God has been poured out in our hearts by the Holy Spirit who was given to us.* (Romans 5:5)

God's love was born out of His will. He chose to love us. He decided before we were even born, before the foundation of the world. His love is not based on chemistry. It is not a feeling. And it does not depend on what we do. Before he created the earth He already knew that Adam would blow it, yet before He created Adam He already planned to show His love by giving His son.

This is the love that God has poured into our hearts. And this is the love we can draw from to love our mates. We love because He loved us first. When you experience God's love you are able to choose the same kind of love in your marriage. When love becomes a choice you are building a marriage that will last forever.

Personal Story: Tom

Maureen has what I call a cast iron will. She wasn't goody two shoes. She was goody steel shoes. Now, when I dated her on and off for six years, I was not a good person. We weren't born again. We weren't saved. But she had made a decision in her heart at a very young age that she would never do anything to hurt the heart of God. I think that gets pretty close to being saved. That was a decision she made. It blows my mind that someone would think that way even before salvation. But not being a particularly good person, I inundated the thoughts and the feelings, trying to override her decision. But I lost. It didn't work. Maureen's decision was an act of her will based on an understanding of God's plan for her. Real love is just as much a decision, no matter what you are feeling.

*The most difficult
years of marriage
are the ones that
follow the wedding.*

9

FORGIVE AND FORGET
DEALING WITH OFFENSE

Set me as a seal upon your heart,
As a seal upon your arm;
For love is as strong as death,
Jealousy as cruel as the grave;
Its flames are flames of fire,
A most vehement flame.
Many waters cannot quench love,
Nor can the floods drown it.
If a man would give for love
All the wealth of his house,
It would be utterly despised.

(Song of Solomon 8:6-7)

These verses are among the most memorable in the Song of Solomon. Throughout the book love is described but here there is a clear attempt to explain its essence.

The bride is the one speaking. The seal was an indication of ownership. The most common form of seal in Canaan was a stamp pressed into clay and placed on the thing being sealed. The bride is asking for ownership of her lover. She is asking him to willingly give himself to her. Symbolically the heart refers to his inner being and the arm to his actions. In other words, she is asking for ownership of his whole person.

The reason for her request is the strength of love. It is stronger than death, endures through the fiercest flame and it can't be bought for any amount of money.

The word "jealousy" is interesting in this context. We usually think of jealousy in a negative sense. The Hebrew word is *qin'a*. It means "a single-minded devotion to something." There are only two relationships in scripture that portray this jealousy in a positive light — God's jealousy toward his people (as in Nahum 1:2 and Zechariah 1:14-17) and in marriage. In both cases it speaks of a desire that will tolerate no rivals, whether the rival be a person, a circumstance or a character trait.

The essence of godly love is that it will survive any kind of pressure.

The word translated "cruel" is *qasa*. It would be better rendered "tenacious." Love is as tenacious as the grave. The essence of godly love is that it will survive any kind of pressure. It is a commitment that does not change.

If this kind of love is a decision, as we have already seen, then it can only be changed by another decision, a decision **not** to love. Unfortunately people make that decision too often because they feel hurt by their mate's words or actions and they are not able to forgive. Real love will overcome. Real love will forgive.

The number one reason for leaving the love walk is unforgiveness. Unforgiveness, if it is not dealt with, becomes offense. Offense turns into anger and anger produces depression. We try to bury it or ignore it but it doesn't go away. It might lay dormant for a time but if we do not deal with it, we will not get rid of it. Someone will say or do something that we perceive as an insult or abuse, and the offense will burst out of us again.

This anger prevents intimacy. It is extremely destructive in a marriage. It undermines the kind of love that husband and wife should have for each other. It is like you keep a can of spray paint handy and every time anyone tries to get too close, you spray them. If you have unresolved issues they come out. When you are full of offense people can't get close to you. You become a bomb ready to explode.

Personal Story: Maureen

When Tom and I first got married we brought this baggage into our marriage, suitcases full of unresolved issues. When we would try to become intimate we would end up opening our suitcases and throwing stuff at each other. And we didn't know why we were acting the way we did.

One issue was with Tom's mother. She left him when he was four years old. So his grandmother raised him and his father remarried. There were some issues there. Tom always had that question in his mind. Would I leave him, too? As long as he had that fear and insecurity it affected our intimacy.

Tom has always been open. We've always been able to sit down and get to the bottom of what the problem is. The Holy Spirit shows us the problem. We give it to Jesus and he washes it away by his blood and then it's gone from our marriage forever.

That's what we did with this issue. Tom had to forgive his mother and God washed the insecurity and fear away and we've never had it in our marriage since.

It is vital, then, that we learn to deal with anger. Scripture tells us that it will produce things that we really don't want. It will have a decidedly negative affect on a marriage. It actually brings in sin.

> *An angry man stirs up strife,*
> *And a furious man abounds in transgression.*
> (Proverbs 29:22)

James gives much the same idea.

> *For the wrath of man does not produce the righteousness of God.* (James 1:20)

To begin with, understand that anger is not sin. It is what you do with your anger that makes the difference.

> *"Be angry, and do not sin": do not let the sun go down on your wrath.*
> (Ephesians 4:26)

Anger is an emotion. Like any emotion it can lead to good or it can lead to bad. Properly managed it will produce greater intimacy in your marriage. If you do not manage it, it will manage you.

First of all we can identify the things that cause anger. Anger is experienced when you feel that you've been wronged by the other person's behavior. They act in an unfair manner or they are disrespectful toward you or they didn't appreciate something you did for them. You expected something from them and didn't get it and the frustration leads to anger.

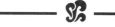

Anger is an emotion. Like any emotion it can lead to good or it can lead to bad.

Anger can also be caused by the loss of something important to you — an object or a dream or a friendship. The failure to fulfill the dreams of your youth can lead to anger.

The goal in managing anger is to take loving actions that will turn the anger in the right direction so that it produces intimacy rather than destruction. You cannot keep a relationship alive for very long when anger remains a part of it. Unresolved anger will kill a relationship.

Anger expresses itself in two ways. It can be explosive, a type of anger that can turn into rage and abuse. Explosive anger can become physical. It often involves throwing things, violent outbursts and yelling.

Anger can also be implosive, meaning it is focused inward where it turns into depression. Implosive anger begins with silence. People withdraw and bottle it up until it turns into resentment, bitterness, offense and eventually it becomes hatred.

They deny that they are mad. When you ask them what is wrong they say, "I'm fine. Nothing's wrong." But they won't talk to you and then they start slamming doors behind them.

Whether explosive or implosive, anger becomes like a looped tape playing in your mind until you are so stuck in the past that you can't live for today. Such anger creates an atmosphere that rules your life. It affects your family and every part of your home and your life.

Personal Story: Maureen

I came from a violent home. Everybody would tap dance around my father when he came home because they didn't want anything to happen.

But you could feel it building and you knew it was going to happen no matter how perfect everyone was. Then the slightest thing would happen and he was gone. The table was thrown up and the spa-

ghetti was all over the place and everybody was running in fear of what was going to happen next.

Some years ago, before he passed away, he came to visit us. One morning we woke up and I could feel the anger and the fear. I could feel it in the air. And I could feel myself wanting to perform because I knew he was going to lose it. I just knew it. I could feel it building all day.

So we were all tap dancing around him because we didn't want the bomb to go off. But everything we did made things worse.

We got to a restaurant and I knew it was going to happen any moment. We were sitting there and he didn't bring in his glasses. So he blamed one of the family. "It's your fault. You're so dumb. You're so stupid." That's how he acted.

The waitress walked by and she put the ketchup on the table a little too hard and that was it. He went berserk.

Once it was over he was extremely sorry. He apologized to her and to everyone at the table. He didn't know why he did it and he always felt bad after it happened. Once it was over and he settled down he was the most loving man imaginable.

But I noticed that even when he apologized to the waitress he wouldn't take responsibility for his actions. He said, "I'm sorry I blew up. I didn't mean it but when you put that ketchup bottle down I lost it." It was still her fault.

My dad was abused by his father. It was a generational thing. But because he wouldn't admit it, because he refused to take responsibility, he was never able to deal with it and it destroyed intimacy in our family.

The patterns of anger need to be broken. If you speak when you are angry you will end up making the best speech you will forever regret. You will say and do things that will severely damage your marriage.

The good news is that these patterns can be broken. The first step is to recognize the destructive potential that anger has. This may prove to be the most difficult part because we generally feel very justified in our anger and, in a twisted kind of way, we even feel better after we have vented. Those around us may have been leveled by the outburst but we feel better. Until we can admit that we have a problem we won't get very far.

Personal Story: Maureen

I never got angry growing up because I never allowed myself to. I didn't want to be like my dad so I would just get away from the situation. In fact I never knew I even had any anger. I was always the calmest person around.

Then I got married. Within the first week I was losing it, going off the deep end, throwing ice cream, lamps, pots and pans. I found anger.

But I had never been like that before. So I knew it couldn't be me. It had to be Tom. I'd accuse him. "You did this to me. You made me into something I don't want to be. It's your fault."

After we became Christians it showed up really bad. It was at its worst when I spent the whole day in the Word. Then I really felt bad because it seemed like even God couldn't help me.

Fortunately Tom did the right thing. He didn't argue with me. He just prayed. And one day I walked into the room and said, "I think I have an anger problem."

Tom said, "Yes, you do." Then he said we should go on a four-day fast and believe God to set me free.

Well, it took several times because it was a generational thing that had quite a hold on my life. The first time we prayed, the Lord showed me something from my childhood. My father used to scare us when we were young, two or three years old. He did things like pulling a nylon stocking over his head and knocking on the bedroom door to wake us up. He thought we were so cute when we were frightened. The Lord showed me that I harbored anger over that.

We prayed and I got free from it but then the anger seemed to come right back. So we fasted and prayed again and the Lord showed us a generational thing. We prayed again and repeated the process one more time after that. Then I was totally free.

ℬ

The first step, then, is to admit the truth to God and to yourself. "I am angry. I'm destructive with my anger and I've mismanaged it."

The hardest part of admitting you have anger is that it is so easy to justify it. "I got hurt. I'm the victim here." You believe you deserve to feel offended.

The truth is that whether your offense is justified or not it will still destroy your marriage. You cannot afford to keep it. Admit you have it so God can begin cleansing it from your life. You have to admit that you are responsible. You have to let it go.

If your mate does or says something that hurts you and he or she apologizes and says, "I'm sorry" and you react in anger then you very likely have some issues to deal with. "You're sorry? Wait a minute. I'm hurt and all you can say is, 'I'm sorry?'" If that is how you react then you better do some self examination. If you don't, you will be stuck in yesterday. You'll be stuck in unforgiveness.

Once you have admitted that there is a problem you can begin developing an effective strategy to break the anger pattern before you get angry. Think back to an event that made you angry. Now consider what you can do to deal with it the next time it happens. Think about a strategy ahead of time.

First of all, when you feel anger rising up in you, call a time out. You and your spouse each need to know that when the adrenaline starts to flow, you have to walk away.

Make it clear that you will continue the conversation when you have calmed down, but until then you don't want to say or do something that will be destructive and that you will regret. Tell your mate, "I need to get away. I need to go for a walk."

Whether your offense is justified or not it will still destroy your marriage.

Walk or go to the gym or do something to give yourself a chance to cool off. As you go, start praying in the Spirit. Get your mind off of the situation. Start thinking about good things until you have calmed down.

Once you are calm you will be in a position to take the next step which is to analyze your anger. Ask yourself some questions about the situation. "Is my anger distorted? Am I just in a bad mood? Is my anger valid? Have I perceived some injustice that really never happened?" This is a time for prayer so that the Holy Spirit can show you the truth about yourself and about the situation.

It may be that God shows you your anger is distorted, that it is really your problem and not your mate's. If that is the case, you need to say it out loud to yourself. Admit it to

God and to yourself that your anger is not valid, that it is self-centered and overly-demanding of your spouse. Ask for forgiveness for a wrong attitude and release your anger to God. He will take it and help you to be loving towards your spouse.

It may be, however, that when you ask yourself these questions you find that the anger is valid. You may find that you really were wronged or treated unjustly. If that is the case then recognize that you have an opportunity to react in a way that is constructive.

You don't want to bury the anger alive and you don't want to simply attack your mate. You may have a right to be angry but remember that the Bible still says to "be angry and do not sin."

It is important to remind yourself of your spouse's good qualities.

The issue has to be discussed with your spouse. If you do it the right way you can build intimacy instead of separation. Think it through before you act. Above all, approach it with kindness, tenderness and a soft voice.

It is important to remind yourself of your spouse's good qualities. Think about what God says concerning him or her. Consider his or her strengths. Tell yourself that your mate loves God and loves you and would not do anything intentionally to hurt you.

The truth is that most people are oblivious to why they do some of the things that they do. They really don't know why they behave that way. They just act out of habitual thought patterns and reactions.

It is essential that you get yourself into a good frame of mind towards your spouse. If you enter the conversation feeling that your mate is a rotten, horrible, thoughtless scoundrel then you will create separation instead of creating intimacy. Remember to speak softly.

A soft answer turns away wrath,
But a harsh word stirs up anger.
(Proverbs 15:1)

There are some things that you can say that will help. Tell your spouse that you know you've mishandled your anger, that you misinterpreted the situation, that you have been wrong but now you want to get it right. Affirm the relationship. "I want to build intimacy between us. I value our covenant. You are the most important thing to me besides God."

This type of approach does not make it sound like you know it all. It does not look like an attack and it will not push your spouse into a defensive posture. Express the possibility that you did not hear it right or that you might not be perceiving it correctly. Tell your spouse that you want to explain what you saw and what you felt and that you then want to hear his or her perspective.

Use "I" statements, not "you" statements. Always remember that your purpose is to build intimacy, not to defend yourself or to attack your spouse.

It is best if you both agree to hear each other's statements without interruption. Ask your mate to allow you to completely express yourself before he or she responds. When you are finished then listen respectfully while your mate talks. Listen without being rude. It is very frustrating to try and share your heart while someone is screaming over the top of you.

The goal is intimacy, not victory.

As you present the situation to your mate limit yourself to one thing. Focus on the matter at hand. Do not use the word "always," as in statements like, "You always do this" or "You always say that." Keep your focus on this one incident.

Point out your mate's good qualities. Emphasize the fact that you might have misunderstood or missed some important information but you are talking now so that you can understand. This approach will help him or her to be open and honest when responding to you. It develops trust.

Never forget that it doesn't matter who wins the argument. The goal is intimacy, not victory.

Be a good listener when it is your turn to listen. You might even want to take some notes. If you want to be understood, then you must learn to understand. The effort on your part will tell your mate that you want to understand him or her and it will help bring healing to the relationship.

When you have finished this step in the process you might come into agreement, in which case one or both of you will apologize and you can take steps to prevent similar mis-understandings in the future. But you might not end up in agreement. What do you do then?

It is essential that you understand that in a healthy re-lationship everyone is encouraged to think for themselves. You are two different people and it is okay for you to see some things differently. That is healthy. What is unhealthy is when you insist on being right and your spouse being wrong. That kind of conflict will destroy intimacy and create distance between you.

You are two different people and it is okay for you to see some things differently.

Men and women are inherently different. Men are more logical. Women are more emotional. Men tell the headlines. Women tell the whole story. Men major on the majors. Women major on everything. Those differences do not have to be an obstacle. When anger is managed properly the dif-ferences, instead of becoming ammunition, become a source of strength.

So far we have talked mainly about what to do if you are the one who has anger. If it is your spouse that has the anger, there are some things you can do to help them. Try not to listen to the abusive words but rather listen to the heart. Try to understand what prompted the anger in the first place. You might need to fast and pray for a time until God gives you some insight.

By not reacting to the anger defensively, by praying

through it, you will be ready to talk when your spouse asks for your help in dealing with the anger. If you let their anger bother you and you react by arguing and defending yourself, you create distance and the intimacy you are trying to establish is destroyed.

The process of getting rid of unresolved anger can be summarized in six steps. First you need to define the anger. Ask the Holy Spirit to help you determine its source — unfulfilled expectations, meanness from another person, fear of loss, loss of dreams or loss of peace of mind. Whatever it is, you need to define it.

The second thing is to allow yourself to face any grief that is attached to it. Grief is a terrible thing to live with. It attaches to you and keeps you constantly reliving the past. When you experience a loss it is natural to feel grief but you have to move on. You cannot let it attach itself to you. Jesus bore our griefs and our sorrows (Isaiah 53:4). You must look to the future and allow God to pour what Psalm 45:7 calls the "oil of gladness" over you. If you do not say good-bye to the grief, you will stay in the past and never move on to your destiny.

There is always something positive that can be derived from any experience.

The third thing is to try to understand your offender. Let the Holy Spirit fill you with compassion so that you can apply mercy to the situation. Try to understand what caused them to act the way they did. When you understand what drives them you will be able to avoid taking it personally and you can keep from becoming offended.

Jesus set the example for us when He was on the cross. Even though they were killing Him, He refused to enter into offense. He recognized that they did not understand why they were acting as they did.

> *Then Jesus said, "Father, forgive them, for they do not know what they do."* (Luke 23:34)

The fourth thing is to look for good in the situation. Find that pearl that can be taken from it. There is always something positive that can be derived from any experience.

> *And we know that all things work together for good to those who love God, to those who are the called according to His purpose.* (Romans 8:28)

The fifth thing is to give it all to Christ. You might want to sit down and write it all out, how you feel, what you think and what you want. Get it out of your mind. Then take the paper, wad it up and throw it in the trash. As it disappears, pray, "Jesus, I surrender to you. I've given it to you and I'm not going to think about it ever again."

The last step is to die to it by the power of the Holy Spirit. You make that choice and it is gone from your life.

As a closing thought to this chapter we need to make one other note. We do not believe that a woman should stay in a situation where her life is in danger. If a husband is physically abusing her she needs to remove herself from that situation for her own safety. Forgiveness does not mean endangering yourself. It does mean letting go of resentment, hatred and bitterness. Do not neglect your personal safety for the pursuit of some religious idea. God called you to forgive but he never intended you to be beaten.

*Even if a man
could understand
women,
he still wouldn't
believe it.*

10

❧

THE SENSUAL SIDE OF LOVE
SEX IN MARRIAGE

How fair and how pleasant you are,
O love, with your delights!
This stature of yours is like a palm tree,
And your breasts like its clusters.
I said, "I will go up to the palm tree.
I will take hold of its branches."
Let now your breasts be like clusters of
    the vine,
The fragrance of your breath like apples,
And the roof of your mouth like the best
    wine.
                    (Song of Solomon 7:6-9)

The Song of Solomon is a blatantly erotic book. This passage is one of the most obvious but it is not the only one. The book is filled with sexual allusions, innuendo and double entendre. You cannot read through it without being made acutely aware of the fact that sensuality is inseparable from a marriage relationship. Love is sensual.

The King bringing his bride into his chambers in 1:4 is pretty clearly a sexual reference. The thirteenth verse of chapter 1 is hard to interpret in any way other than sexual.

A bundle of myrrh is my beloved to me,
That lies all night between my breasts.
(Song of Solomon 1:13)

Verse 16 refers to their bed as "verdant" or "green," meaning it is full of life, an allusion to an active, living sex life. The raisins and apples of 2:5 were considered to be aphrodisiacs in the ancient world. In 3:4 the bride brings her lover into the house of her mother, another reference to lovemaking. The description of the bride in chapter 4 is very sensual. The drinking of intoxicating beverages is likened to the intoxication of love (1:2; 5:1; 7:9; 8:2). In the last of those verses the bride even speaks of him drinking her juices.

I would cause you to drink of spiced wine,
Of the juice of my pomegranate.
(Song of Solomon 8:2)

In some branches of Judaism young people are not allowed to read the Song of Solomon until they are engaged and ready to marry. Its eroticism is considered to be too strong. It is not inappropriate, however. It is not lewd or pornographic, in spite of its sensuality. Rather, it is sexuality redeemed from that which is inappropriate, portrayed in all of its passion and purity as God intended it to be in marriage.

For most people sexuality needs redeeming. Our understanding of sex has been formed from some very questionable sources. Most of it has come from the coat hall when we were in the fifth or sixth grade, or from sneaking looks at magazines or from a few books we picked up along the way, or from things we overheard our parents say. It has been a hodgepodge of information with very little depth.

You might learn from counseling, either Christian or secular, but in either case a psychologist may have worse hang-ups than you. You don't know what their background is or how biased their information will be. Friends are even less reliable since they might have a worse history or background than you, especially if they were sexually abused. You can buy a lot of books. Some are good but most are not. They are usually done with a personal bias because they are written from only one perspective. When a man writes a book on sexuality it will have a male bias. When a woman writes one it will have a female bias.

For most people sexuality needs redeeming.

The Word of God is the only genuinely reliable source for learning about human sexuality. We have already discussed the fact that God is both male and female. We can trust Him to have a truly impartial perspective.

The church's attitude toward sex has generally been less than redemptive. Some of our forefathers had some strange ideas about it. Many of them were great men of God and we owe much of our Christian heritage to them, but in the area of sexuality they often appear to have been blinded by their religious perceptions.

Generally, by the second century, sex came to be viewed as the sin that caused the fall of man from grace. Nearly every church leader followed this pattern.

Ignatius, a second century theologian, is well known to us for his inspired leadership and his writings in the early church. He was one of the most respected church leaders in the world from the generation following the apostles. But he taught that Adam and Eve were virgins until they were expelled from the Garden of Eden and that childbirth was Eve's punishment for having sex. Of course God had commanded them to fill the earth, a difficult thing to do if they were never to have sex. Yet this teaching became a standard part of the religious training of the time.

St. Jerome, in the fourth century, is best remembered for his conviction that the Word of God needed to be accessible to all men, so he labored to translate it into Latin, the common language of his time. The result was the translation called the Vulgate, which means "common." Like Ignatius, Jerome was one of the most influential men of his time. It is hard to find men in history with a greater respect and love for the Bible. But Jerome taught that the only way women could overcome Eve's sin of having sex was to live the life of a virgin. He once proclaimed that the only saving grace of marriage was found in the possibility that such union could produce more virgins.

In that time, if a person wanted to be right with God he would swear never to have sex. Women were put into convents and men into monasteries. At the age of puberty, as early as seven or eight, boys were placed in monasteries so that they would not be troubled by human sexuality. Of course perversions, especially homosexuality, became extreme problems in those settings because you can't suppress what God created. You can pervert it but you can't suppress it.

St. Augustine lived around 400 A.D. He was perhaps the most influential man in church history with the exceptions of the apostle Paul and Jesus. He wrote so many books on theology that we could not even begin to summarize them here. But a few observations will give an idea of the impact he had.

You can't suppress what God created. You can pervert it but you can't suppress it.

The basic beliefs that we have today about original sin and the sin nature are primarily those articulated by Augustine. This man of God believed that the original sin was sex, that Adam and Eve copulated by the tree and God got mad. He taught that sex was a carnal weakness and in order to avoid it he abandoned his lover and his child, left them to scrape out a poverty-level existence on their own, and he entered full-time ministry. It apparently never occurred to him that God might be pleased if he took responsibility for the family he had created or the child God had given him.

It was around this time that celibacy became a requirement for priesthood, based on Paul's statement to the Corinthians.

> *But I say this as a concession, not as a commandment. For I wish that all men were even as I myself. But each one has his own gift from God, one in this manner and another in that. But I say to the unmarried and to the widows: It is good for them if they remain even as I am; but if they cannot exercise self-control, let them marry. For it is better to marry than to burn with passion.* (1 Corinthians 7:6-9)

It is interesting that the church could derive a command against sex from this scripture when Paul so clearly says that it is not a command, but simply advice about how to handle your passion. If you are going to be in the ministry your family will always come first. It says that if you are already married then stay that way.

> *Are you bound to a wife? Do not seek to be loosed.* (1 Corinthians 7:27)

But if you insist on putting the ministry first, then you should just stay single.

> *He who is unmarried cares for the things of the Lord — how he may please the Lord. But he who is married cares*

about the things of the world — how he may please his wife. (1 Corinthians 7:32-33)

If married couples never had sex it would be impossible to fulfill the command in Genesis to multiply. Other instructions Paul gave wouldn't make any sense either.

Do not deprive one another except with consent for a time, that you may give yourselves to fasting and prayer; and come together again so that Satan does not tempt you because of your lack of self-control. (1 Corinthians 7:5)

Of course, these leaders in the church were not stupid, even if they had some strange ideas. They knew that if everyone in the world stopped having sex it wouldn't be long before there were no people left. By the twelfth and thirteenth centuries sex was considered to be appropriate only for procreation. Permission had to be obtained from the priest before a married couple was allowed to have sex. There is record of one couple who didn't engage in sex for thirty years because they believed their abstinence would please God.

During the Inquisition of the thirteenth and fourteenth centuries, sexual attraction was noted as an indication of witchcraft. It was believed that a beautiful woman had an evil power over men that came from the Garden of Eden and the sin of sex and therefore must be a demon. Any man who was so attracted, especially if he was a religious leader, could report such a woman to the magistrates and they would try her immediately. Thousands were killed.

This mentality carried over for at least three more centuries and became part of the Puritan thinking in early America that contributed to the New England witch trials in the 1600's.

On October 31, 1517, Martin Luther nailed his Ninety-Five Theses to the door of the Wittenberg church and sparked a movement that still continues today. With the advent of the Reformation some significant changes took place. The invention of the Gutenberg printing press meant that for the first time, it was possible for the common people to get their hands on the Bible and read the Word of God for themselves. Revival broke out across northern Europe in the arts and music and literature, in fact in all of life. Much of the repression of earlier centuries began to break up.

When monks and priests started renouncing their vows and getting married Martin Luther was forced to reconsider his beliefs about marriage. He concluded from the direction in Genesis 1:28 to multiply and fill the earth that marriage was actually a biblical command.

In 1525, twelve nuns from a nunnery in Nimbschen, Germany sent a message to Luther. They were virtually prisoners in the nunnery. One man had already been executed for trying to help them escape. They had secretly obtained some of Luther's tracts and wondered if he would help them. He arranged for a senior citizen named Leonard Kopp to pull off the escape. Kopp regularly delivered barrels of smoked herring to the cloister. One day he managed to exchange twelve barrels of herring for twelve barrels that were supposedly empty but which in fact each contained a nun. Two days later twelve nuns turned up on Luther's doorstep.

He felt obligated to not only find them jobs but to find them husbands as well. He eventually helped all of them but one, Katherine von Bora. When every effort on her behalf failed, Luther finally married her himself. She was outspoken, headstrong, independent and argumentative, but they were both committed to the principles of a biblical marriage and ultimately they became models of what husband and wife could do as a team.

Martin Luther was forced to reconsider his beliefs about marriage.

We would like to say that the religious bondage that so affected marriage in the Middle Ages is now history, but these attitudes of restriction and control still show up today in church rules about how to dress, about not wearing makeup or jewelry, and in rules about movies and dancing. All of these things have affected our views of human sexuality.

It is not surprising that many have reacted by running in the opposite direction. The Reformation saw spiritual freedom burst onto the scene but at the same time the Renaissance saw a proliferation in art and philosophy of attention to the flesh. Voltaire expressed it in the form of early humanism. Everything is okay. There is no boundary, no standard, no code of ethics that matters. Perversions abounded. Homosexuality was more readily accepted.

The arts reflected the trend. "The Garden of Delight," for example, was a painting depicting every form of sexual perversion known to the artist, including sex with animals. The result of all this is a society today that says anything is okay at the same time that much of the church says that nothing is okay.

The truth is that sex is God-given. It is intended for marriage. It is meant for procreation but it is also meant for fun. Sexual intimacy is the greatest high that our bodies were designed for. It is two people coming together as one flesh to produce a child, which is really one flesh of the two. But sex, and particularly the climax of sexual intercourse, is also the closest thing we can experience on this earth to being in heaven. Sex is fun, joyful, fulfilling and important to the marriage.

> *Sexual intimacy is the greatest high that our bodies were designed for.*

With this background in mind we should make note of a few things concerning sex. Sex is a causative factor in a good marriage, not the result of a good marriage. When emotional needs are met, sex is good. If more men understood this they would meet the emotional needs of their wives and their sex would improve. You cannot be effectively one without sex in the marriage.

Let the husband render to his wife the affection due her, and likewise also the wife to her husband. The wife does not have authority over her own body, but the husband does. And likewise the husband does not have authority over his own body but the wife does. (1 Corinthians 7:3-4)

Paul is talking specifically about sex. It is true that these verses have spiritual applications. No one can pray as effectively over the wife as her husband and no one can pray as effectively over the husband as his wife.

But Paul is still talking about sex. The next verse tells them not to deprive one another. Your body is not your own. It belongs to your mate. Without regular sex and good sex in marriage, temptation may come your way. Biblical sex means all sexual activity between husband and wife that they agree to is uncontrolled by boundaries that hinder mutual pleasure.

Marriage is honorable among all, and the bed undefiled; but fornicators and adulterers God will judge. (Hebrews 13:4)

In other words any sexual activity that husband and wife agree to, within the confines of their own relationship, is okay. One does not force the other. That is never God's intent. Neither do they include other people in their sexual union.

As with every aspect of marriage, good sex is the art of meeting your mate's needs. There is an old saying in psychology that sex is ten percent of a good marriage and ninety percent of a bad one. By paying attention to its importance, the sexual relationship will contribute to the quality of the whole marriage. It cannot be ignored any more than any other aspect of relationship.

*Girls who fall
in love at first
sight later wish
they had taken
a second look.*

11

IS IT ABOUT ME?
MEETING SEXUAL NEEDS

My beloved is white and ruddy,
Chief among ten thousand.
His head is like the finest gold;
His locks are wavy,
And black as a raven.
His eyes are like doves
By the rivers of waters,
Washed with milk,
And fitly set.
His cheeks are like a bed of spices,
Banks of scented herbs.
His lips are lilies,
Dripping liquid myrrh.
His hands are rods of gold
Set with beryl.
His body is carved ivory
Inlaid with sapphires.
His legs are pillars of marble
Set on bases of fine gold.
His countenance is like Lebanon,
Excellent as the cedars.
His mouth is most sweet,
Yes, he is altogether lovely.

This is my beloved,
And this is my friend,
O daughters of Jerusalem!.
(Song of Solomon 5:10-16)

You need to physically look your best. Do all that you can to be attractive for your mate. The groom in the Song of Solomon certainly looked good.

In this passage we see how the bride perceived him. His hair was combed. His cologne smelled good. He was strong; he obviously had been working out. Even his breath smelled good. He took great care with his appearance. He was a very considerate lover.

There are a few problems that are quite common in marriages. Most of them are not that hard to fix if you recognize them and make a little effort to do so.

One that we see on a regular basis is in this area of desirability. It is interesting how often you see a husband or a wife get a divorce and a week later they look ten times better than they ever did when they were married. They dress better. They have makeup on. They're on a diet and working out. They have to look good so they can get somebody else. It would make so much more sense to look better now and keep the one you're with.

The groom in Song of Solomon looked good and it is obvious that at least part of that was due to an effort to keep looking good. He obviously did some things on a regular basis to keep himself fit.

His bride looked good, too. When he describes her he takes notice of the curves of her figure, her breasts, her eyes, neck and her hair.

> *How beautiful are your feet in sandals,*
> *O prince's daughter!*
> *The curves of your thighs are like jewels,*
> *The work of the hands of a skillful work-*
> *man.*
> *Your navel is a rounded goblet;*
> *It lacks no blended beverage.*
> *Your waist is a heap of wheat*
> *Set about with lilies.*
> *Your two breasts are like two fawns,*
> *Twins of a gazelle.*
> *Your neck is like an ivory tower,*
> *Your eyes like the pools in Heshbon*
> *By the gate of Bath Rabbim.*
> *Your nose is like the tower of Lebanon*
> *Which looks toward Damascus.*
> *Your head crowns you like Mount Carmel,*
> *And the hair of your head is like purple;*
> *A king is held captive by your tresses.*
> (Song of Solomon 7:1-5)

She has taken care of herself. Verse 8 tells us that her breath was good, too. She used perfume so she smelled good.

While the king is at his table,
My spikenard sends forth its fragrance.
A bundle of myrrh is my beloved to me,
That lies all night between my breasts.
(Song of Solomon 1:12-13)

In chapter 4 she is described in terms of fragrance.

A garden enclosed
Is my sister, my spouse,
A spring shut up,
A fountain sealed.
Your plants are an orchard of pomegran-
ates
With pleasant fruits,
Fragrant henna with spikenard,
Spikenard and saffron,
Calamus and cinnamon,
With all trees of frankincense,
Myrrh and aloes,
With all the chief spices.
(Song of Solomon 4:12-14)

In 5:5 her hands drip with myrrh.

In 3:6 it is the groom who is perfumed. All of these verses refer to smelling good. It is biblical to use perfume, not just to cover up body odors, but to enhance desirability.

You need to dress nicely. Not much is directly said in

Song of Solomon about clothing but what is said is significant. The bride in particular must have been dressed in a manner intended to catch the attention of her husband. We can surmise that from the descriptions he gives of her appearance, but other elements tell us the same thing. Four times mention is made of her veil (4:1, 3; 5:7; 6:7). Veils were not universally worn in the culture of Solomon's time. The veil was something intentionally worn to hide beauty while increasing desire. The fact that it is mentioned in the way it is tells us that her intention was to look enticing to him.

She wore jewelry.

> *Your cheeks are lovely with ornaments,*
> *Your neck with chains of gold.*
> (Song of Solomon 1:10)

And it was jewelry that must have been very beautiful.

> *You have ravished my heart*
> *With one look of your eyes,*
> *With one link of your necklace.*
> (Song of Solomon 4:9)

It is an expression of your love for your mate when you do your best to be desirable, to look good, to smell good and to dress well. Such consideration should be a way of life.

Personal Story: Tom

My wife gets up every single morning for the past thirty-six years, no matter what morning it is, and showers, gets dressed, puts on her makeup and does her hair. Every day for thirty-six years she has looked like a million dollars.

I've had to work on not looking like a slob on Saturdays when I'm off work. I've had to work on that diligently. On my day off I'm going to work in the yard and sweat a little so I just wear my flip flops and some torn up cut offs and a T-shirt I should have retired a long time ago. Gradually I have learned that I need to look good for her. I need to look good every morning and smell good every morning. It's something she does for me and I do it for her.

There are a few things women should know about men that will help them understand their husbands and how they can better meet their needs. Most importantly, wives, you should understand the frailty of the male ego. A man gives the appearance of being the protector, the masculine strength of the home. But that ego needs to be built up by his wife, especially in the area of sexuality. The male ego is the weakest part of his makeup. He needs to be assured that he is a great lover. The bride in the Song of Solomon constantly affirms his masculinity.

*My beloved is like a gazelle or a young
stag.*
(Song of Solomon 2:9)

Ladies, you can either make or break your husband's sexuality by the power of your words. If you consistently nag and criticize his character, you will, over time, produce an inability in him to perform sexually. You can make him a great lover by talking about what your needs are so that he can do better than he has done, but be careful how you approach it. You always want to encourage. A man must be reassured by the one person he trusts and feels loved by that he is a great lover.

A little response to a man's advances is good. Watching television over his shoulder is not conducive to a sexual encounter. Reading a novel off to the side will not encourage him. An occasional "ooh" and "ahh" will go a long way toward greater sexual compatibility.

> *An occasional "ooh" and "ahh" will go a long way toward greater sexual compatibility.*

Premature ejaculation and impotence are nearly always psychological. Occasionally there is a medical problem but most of the time it is easily overcome by the woman encouraging the man through words and by physical response. Too much negative input can make you undesirable to your mate. For a healthy sexual relationship learn to encourage. Never mother. What man wants sex with his mother?

There are some specific things men need to remember about women, too. Men's failure to show affection before and during the sexual act will cause sexual incompatibility. Gentleness, kindness, caring, tenderness and encouragement are all critical prior to the act of sex, during the act of sex and after the act of sex. Men, you should never hurry. Women need to feel loved and secure in the relationship. Having trust is absolutely essential.

The kind of foreplay that women need goes on all the time in a healthy relationship.

The husband needs to be emotionally involved in foreplay. Emotional foreplay can begin days before the sexual encounter. In fact it should never really stop. When a man becomes emotionally intimate with his wife by hearing her heart, hearing her needs, by listening intensely, becoming part of her communication and getting connected emotionally, their sex life will improve dramatically. Women have an emotional makeup that men must connect to emotionally, develop security in and encourage. Men, if you give an ounce in this area you will get back a ton in response. You must seek how to satisfy her.

The kind of foreplay that women need goes on all the time in a healthy relationship. It is those gentle romantic hugs that are not sexual. It is those words of encouragement that say, "I love you and I care about you." It is the little gifts that you give. It is about what you invest in the giving process of making her feel loved, important and secure. Emotional needs come first. Sex comes second.

A good sexual relationship requires that both husband and wife have a good knowledge of each other's bodies and know what arouses each other. Communicate. Talk about it. What does he like? What does she like?

Men are aroused visually more than women and they are aroused much more quickly. Women, if your husband is in bed waiting for you and you emerge from the bathroom wearing nothing, it is possible he will be interested in sex just from that image. At that point, if you say you are too tired, you may have him scratching the headboard the rest of the night or taking a cold shower.

Women are aroused more slowly and feel love by words and touch. They like caressing and foreplay nearly as much as the sex act itself. Take your time. Physical foreplay is important to build arousal in both men and women.

Emotional needs come first.

Sex comes second.

Plan time for sex but remember that spontaneity can enhance the sexual experience. Spontaneity might mean the kitchen table when the kids are in school. It could be almost anywhere and at times that were not planned.

Before we conclude our discussion of sexuality we need to consider some of the things that hinder a good sexual relationship. Unfaithfulness to the marriage bed will have a detrimental effect. Unfaithfulness includes many things. Pornography is unfaithfulness. Masturbation, fantasizing and artificial stimulation are unfaithfulness. Sex with another partner or adding another partner to your marriage bed is unfaithfulness. Anything that produces sexual gratification outside the marriage bed is infidelity and unfaithfulness and it hinders becoming one flesh.

Past relationships can hinder a current relationship. They developed spiritual, emotional and physical bonds that affect your marriage today. There was a giving and receiving that produced fantasies and unreal expectations that create dissatisfaction with your present mate.

This is not something you should share with your spouse. In fact you should **not** share it. But you should pray through it. Those past bonds need to be severed so that you can give one hundred percent of your body, soul and spirit to your present mate. When you do, there will be a significant change in your marriage.

An effective way to pray is to imagine the person or the episode or circumstance. See yourself give back to them a beautiful package that has been wrapped with a bow. See yourself receive back from them a beautiful package that you had given to them. Don't make it an ugly package because it is something that was part of you. Make that exchange and then picture Jesus, however you envision him, stepping between you and that past relationship and cutting every spiritual line, tie and connection off of your life. The moment you do that, both you and the other person will be free to go on with your relationships. Jesus the Word died for our sins and sickness but he also died for griefs and sorrows. Therefore the truth can free you from past encounters. God forgives and forgets and we need to do the same.

Another hindrance is a poor relationship with your parents. The Bible makes it very clear about what kind of attitude we should have.

> *Honor your father and your mother,*
> *that your days may be long upon the land.*
> (Exodus 20:12)

You have a responsibility to love those that gave you life, even if they were the pits, because you want to have a long life. That means that you have to forgive them for sexual abuse, emotional abuse and physical abuse. There are no qualifying clauses to this commandment. You are to honor them. That doesn't mean you have to hang out with them. They still may not be friendly to you, but if you do not honor and forgive them it will affect every part of your life, including your sexual relationship with your spouse.

Personal Story: Tom
My mother left and abandoned me at the age of four. Now we're getting reestablished after more than thirty years. God is restoring that relationship. But as a result of her leaving I always had a fear in

our early days of marriage that women abandon. Therefore you can't trust them. As a result I had extreme jealousy. We were in a charismatic church twenty-five years ago and the pastor said, "Everybody go around and hug somebody."

I leaned over to Maureen and said, "If any guy hugs you I'm going to drop him right here. Just so you know."

Well, God protected me even in my sin. Nobody came near us. But those were areas that I had to get over — insecurity and loss. It was created by my parent and it would become destructive to the relationship. So I had to deal with that issue and forgive my mother so that I wouldn't carry it into my marriage.

Still another hindrance is fear of rejection. Hatred of yourself or of your body can cause a fear of being rejected in a sexual encounter. If you don't like your body or how you look there are some things you can do to change your appearance, but you still need to love yourself.

Wrong attitudes about sex, from home, friends, family, movies or sexual abuse at an early age can hinder sexuality in a couple of ways. It can cause frigidity or a fear of sex, even in marriage, because it is too terrifying and brings back too much memory of pain.

On the other hand, it can also produce promiscuousness with no boundaries in sexual encounters. Extremely promiscuous women often were victims of sexual abuse from their fathers, uncles or some other relative. As a result, they feel worthless and all they do is consistently seek a father's approval through sexual encounters with other men. It becomes a driving force. All of these things have to be overcome. There has to be forgiveness.

Sexual relationships can be hindered when love is transferred from the mate to children. Sometimes when the marriage relationship is not going well we tend to dump all of our love into our kids instead of our mate. The result may be closer bonding with our children but it creates jealousy in the mate and does not help the marriage at all.

There is one other significant area of sexuality that needs to be considered. As we pass the age of 40 up to about 55 or so we gradually begin to experience changes in hormone levels. They can create changes in sexual desire as well.

In men it is usually associated with what has come to be known as mid-life crisis. Sexual desire may start to diminish. Other symptoms include anger, irritability, tiredness and difficulty gaining or maintaining an erection.

Frequently a man with these problems will blame his wife, claiming that she no longer excites him. He suddenly thinks the answer is a sports car and a younger wife. But the problem is something internal, a physiological change.

A woman goes through similar changes during menopause. Her body undergoes significant chemical changes. She experiences extreme mood swings and cries over the simplest things. She can be tired, angry and irritable. She might be unhappy one moment and extremely happy the next. As with men the changes are primarily chemical and internal. DHEA levels are dropping. Progesterone, estrogen and testosterone levels are changing. It is a physical reaction.

For both men and women there are solutions. For women, if you gain weight too rapidly and you are tired all the time, your thyroid might be inactive. You can get prescriptions to correct that. Low testosterone levels will lower sexual desire. DHEA is critical for sexuality. Women need 10 mg per day. They need 1 to 3 mg of melatonin each evening before bed for the best sleep. Ginkgo biloba is a memory enhancer. Progesterone and estrogen can also be supplemented through prescriptions.

Men need many of the same things as they age. They should take 25-50 mg per day of DHEA. Testosterone levels can be supplemented. The same problems with the thyroid that women have might also be experienced by men. There are growth hormones available by prescription. Men also need melatonin and ginkgo biloba as much as women.

Greater sexual stimulation is needed as we grow older. We need more preparation, more emotional investment, more communication, more foreplay, more touching and more time allowed. In every respect it is important to take good care of yourself and of your mate. There is no age limit for love stories.

*Some people
believe in dreams
until they
marry one.*

———————————————

12

℘

MOVING PAST THE PAST
FREEDOM IN MARRIAGE

Scarcely had I passed by them,
When I found the one I love.
I held him and would not let him go,
Until I had brought him to the house of
my mother,
And into the chamber of her who con-
ceived me.
(Song of Solomon 3:4)

In many ways this is one of the more peculiar verses in the Song of Solomon. The bride again appears very aggressive in this relationship, hardly the passive stereotype that is usually held up as a godly woman. She grabs her lover and drags him off to the privacy of the bedroom. The peculiar fact, however, is that she intends to make love in her mother's bedroom. The same reference is made again later.

I would lead you and bring you
Into the house of my mother,
She who used to instruct me.
I would cause you to drink of spiced wine,
Of the juice of my pomegranate.
(Song of Solomon 8:2)

This imagery was common in the ancient world. It symbolized a place of security but it also denoted the place of mothers in arranging marriages for their daughters. The importance of the mother's place is validated in scripture. In Ruth 1:8-9 Naomi encourages her two daughters-in-law to return to their "mother's house." Isaac and Rebekah consummate their marriage in his mother's tent (Genesis 24:67). It is Solomon's mother who crowns him on the day of his marriage (Song of Solomon 3:11).

> *When you get married you are not just marrying another person.*

Such references may be simply a description of Hebrew culture but they also hint at a very important consideration. When you get married you are not just marrying another person. That person cannot be separated from his or her background and family history. We all inherit many values and attitudes from our parents. Some of them are good and some of them are not. The Song of Solomon recognizes this connection.

The good things that we bring from our families don't need a great deal of comment. They are good, so we do not worry much about them. It is the bad things, the baggage, that we need to be concerned about. There are generational curses that we need to get free of.

The Old Testament gives us a picture of entering the Promised Land, the land that flows with milk and honey. This land is our new heritage, a picture of where God wants us to live. The problem is that there are enemies in the land and they are determined to keep you from experiencing the freedom that you should have. They are squatters occupying your inheritance and they have to go. Fortunately, God said he would drive them out.

> *When the LORD your God brings you into the land which you go to possess, and has cast out many nations before you, the Hittites and the Girgashites and the Amorites and the Canaanites and the Perizzites and the Hivites and the Jebusites, seven nations greater and mightier than you, and when the LORD your God delivers them over to you, you shall conquer them and utterly destroy them. You shall make no covenant with them nor show mercy to them. Nor shall you make marriages with them. You shall not give your daughter to their son nor take their daughter for your son. For they will turn your sons away from following Me, to serve other gods.* (Deuteronomy 7:1-4)

These nations represent a variety of things that seem to be impossible to get rid of. If we did a detailed study of these nations we would find that each one symbolized one of the tools that the enemy uses to prevent you from entering into God's promises. The Hittites represented fear. The Girgashites were a picture of double mindedness. The Amorites represented pride. The Canaanites were a type of materialistic attitudes, the Perizzites immorality. The Hivites pictured deception and the Jebusites depression.

These are all the areas that can be passed on from generation to generation. They can manifest themselves in a variety of ways. They can be overeating. They can be lack of self-control. They can be anger or lust. You swear that you will never do something again and then you do.

But the Word says that God will deliver them over to you. By his power, the power of his Word, you will conquer them. You can't live with them. They have to be driven out.

> *But if you do not drive out the inhabitants of the land from before you, then it shall be that those whom you let remain shall be irritants in your eyes and thorns in your sides, and they shall harass you in the land where you dwell.* (Numbers 33:55)

They may be greater and mightier than you, but the Word says that God will drive them out.

Before you became born again you were under the curse. You lived with the generational curses that your family embraced. You were like an old man who goes out and collects garbage. The old man loved garbage. He brought it home and filled his house with it. That garbage has been accumulating now for generations. Your forefathers collected it and passed it on to you. That garbage is now part of your life because that is your family. You were born with it.

Then you became born again and your old man died. But you still have all the garbage. And it has to be cleaned out. But if God dealt with it all at once it would be overwhelming. So he takes it a little at a time.

> *And the LORD your God will drive out those nations before you little by little; you will be unable to destroy them at once, lest the beasts of the field become too numerous for you.* (Deuteronomy 7:22)

So the grace of the Holy Spirit covers you and your house. But then one day he goes into a room and points to something and says, "It's time to deal with this."

You may not want to get rid of your improprieties, though. So you hang on to them. But when it is time for them to go, grace doesn't cover them anymore. They have to go.

Deuteronomy says that we are not to make a covenant with the improprieties. We are not to bind ourselves to them or to become one with them. We are not to expect the rest of the family to love them. We are to get free of them.

Deuteronomy 7:3 expresses it by saying that you are not to give your children to them in marriage. When you con-

tinue to embrace the curses, that is exactly what you are doing — marrying them to your children. You are saying, "This
curse is okay. It can stay in our
home." And you pass it on to your
children.

❧

Generational blessings are even more powerful than the curses.

We are first generation
Christians, the first ones in our
families to know Jesus. That means
that we have a responsibility to take
these territories so that we do not
pass the curses on to our children.
We want them to live in the blessing.

The curses may be poverty or laziness or sickness. Your
family may have a history of divorce. The good thing is that
generational blessings are even more powerful than the curses.
When you break free of the curse and start living in the blessing then you will begin to pass blessing on to your children.

❧

Personal Story: Maureen

*Tom and I both came from a family that had a
history of divorce. His mother and father were divorced. My forefathers had been divorced all the
way back and remarried two or three times. When
we married we were under a curse of divorce. It's
what our forefathers handed over to the enemy.*

*But God called us to build strong homes and
families. Well, we had what we thought was a pretty*

good marriage. He did his thing and I did mine. He sat at the back of the church and I sat in the front and we were happy.

I was used to being independent. I was from a big family and everybody did their own thing. Tom was an only child until he was eleven and he was used to doing his own thing.

So all of a sudden Tom said, "It's time for us to have a kingdom marriage."

Everywhere I went someone was saying to me, "God's going to start working on your marriage." I thought our marriage was pretty good. But Tom said, "Honey, I think we need to start praying a half an hour a day in the spirit over our marriage."

Well, nothing was going on. We weren't in any big battlefield or anything. We were fine, so I said, "Okay." We started praying half an hour.

But as soon as we started to pray it was like I opened the door of hell itself — the curse of divorce. It was just like I put myself in the darkest room ever. There was so much fear and darkness, overwhelmingly dark and bad. I only lasted about two seconds and I was ready to stop. I wished I hadn't opened that door. I was seeing into the unseen world. We were under a curse and didn't even know it.

Tom prayed for a half hour. I didn't say anything but the next day I was all emotional — and I'm not an emotional person. I called my girlfriend and said, "Oh, this is terrible, horrible. I don't want to do this. This is not God."

Tom came home and I told him what happened. "This is not God. There's no grace on this."

Of course Tom said, "This is God and you're going to have to trust me. We're going to pray this through."

So I said, "Okay. I trust you." So every day we prayed in the spirit for a half hour. We made a commitment we were going to pray off all that darkness that was in the unseen world. We were going to pray until we saw Jesus in our marriage.

It took two weeks — only two weeks. As we were praying the Holy Spirit kept showing us different situations to take dominion over. As soon as we saw it we prayed over it, turned it over to God and moved on.

And then one day we were praying and the presence of God came and Jesus was there. The curse of divorce was gone.

God called us to build strong families. The devil was waiting for the opportunity to recreate divorce. But we prayed the curse off of our own marriage. After we did that it was interesting that we could feel that unconditional love just clothe our family and our home from that day on.

*Making marriage
work is like a farm.
You start working
it all over again
each morning.*

————————

✿ HAPPILY EVER AFTER

Solomon had a vineyard at Baal Hamon;
He leased the vineyard to keepers;
Everyone was to bring for its fruit
A thousand silver coins.
My own vineyard is before me.
You, O Solomon, may have a thousand,
And those who tend its fruit two hundred.
(Song of Solomon 8:11-12)

Solomon had his vineyard and it was successful and pro-ductive. He leased it and it brought in substantial profits for him.

What is of interest to us in this passage is the bride's vineyard. At the beginning of the Song of Solomon, the bride was being forced to work in the vineyards of others. In 1:6 she said, "But my own vineyard I have not kept." Now we are at the end of the story and her own vineyard is before her. What true love has done is to bring her dreams to fulfillment. The Song of Solomon is a love story with a happy ending.

"And they lived happily ever after." That would be the fitting conclusion to a happy love story today. Of course such an ending is only possible for those who base their marriage on the never-ending and unchangeable principles of God's Word. It is those principles that we have presented to you.

Each area we have discussed is significant. We have seen that men and women are different but differences are what give strength to the relationship. We have seen that there is an equality in marriage that does not make either the husband or the wife a slave but rather leads to freedom and life.

We have seen that healthy communication requires learning to hear what your mate is really saying. Misunderstanding can arise when perceptions are wrong. Learning to speak your mate's love language is essential.

We have seen that healthy love has to have maturity in the practical considerations of everyday life, especially financial responsibility. Secure finances take a tremendous amount of strain off of the relationship.

We have seen that a healthy marriage absolutely requires good, open and honest communication. Where needs are not expressed they are not likely to be met.

We have seen that real love requires both husband and wife to change and to grow. No one is perfect. Thus no marriage is perfect. There needs to be a willingness to change over time.

We have seen that love, if it is to last for a lifetime, must be a decision, not a feeling. The emotions of love will follow the decision but the decision needs to be the ultimate foundation of the relationship for it to be healthy. Love requires commitment.

We have seen that a healthy sexual relationship is necessary. Physical love is an integral part of being spiritual.

We have seen that God can deliver us and that he desires to deliver us from the bad habits, attitudes and decisions of the past. A healthy marriage means becoming free from generational curses.

We have discussed many details of how marriage works. When we look at all of them, however, we can summarize every aspect of a healthy marriage in a couple of statements. In every way, the marriage is not about you. It is about your spouse. It means giving of yourself for the good of your mate.

The bride in the Song of Solomon achieved her dream. That speaks well of the groom.

It means laying down your life for the life of the one you have chosen to love. It means being willing to die to yourself so that your mate can fulfill his or her God-given destiny.

Ultimately you can measure your personal success in marriage by the success of your mate. If a husband is all that God created him to be then it is an indication of his wife's success as a wife. If a wife is all that God created her to be then it is an indication of her husband's success as a husband.

It is typical of how God does things that following this approach to relationships is the only way that you will ever find fulfillment and satisfaction. The bride in the Song of Solomon achieved her dream. That speaks well of the groom.

Our desire for you is that you learn these principles and apply them to your marriage. Our desire is for you to truly develop a love story in your marriage. Our prayer is that your story ends with, "And they lived happily ever after."

BIBLIOGRAPHY

Bilezikian, Gilbert. *Community 101, Reclaiming the Local Church as Community of Oneness*. Zondervan PublishingHouse. Grand Rapids, Michigan. 1997. 207 pgs.

Chapman, Gary. *The Five Love Languages, How to Express Heartfelt Commitment to Your Mate*. Northfield Publishing. Chicago. 1995. 204 pgs.

Dillenberger, John (Editor). *Martin Luther: Selections from his Writings*. Anchor Books, Doubleday & Company. Garden City, New York. 1961. 526 pgs.

France, R.T. *Women in the Church's Ministry: A Test Case for Biblical Interpretation*. William B. Eerdmans Publishing Company. Grand Rapids, Michigan. 1995. 96 pgs.

Fromm, Erich. *The Art of Loving*. Harper & Row. New York. 1956. 130 pgs.

Good, Joseph. *Rosh HaShanah and the Messianic Kingdom to Come, A Messianic Jewish Interpretation of the Feast of Trumpets*. Hatikva Ministries. Port Arthur, Texas. 1989. 197 pgs.

Hagin, Kenneth E. *The Woman Question*. Faith Library Publications. Tulsa, Oklahoma. 1983. 66 pgs.

Longman III, Tremper. *Song of Songs*. William B. Eerdmans Publishing Company. Grand Rapids, Michigan. 2001. 238 pgs.

Moir, Anne and David Jessel. *Brain Sex: The Real Difference Between Men & Women*. Dell. New York. 1992. 242 pgs.

Smalley, Gary. *Making Love Last Forever*. Word Publishing. 1996.

Torjesen, Karen Jo. *When Women Were Priests: Women's Leadership in the Early Church & the Scandal of Their Subordination in the Rise of Christianity*. HarperSanFranscsco. 1993. 278 pgs.

Treat, Wendy. *Battle of the Sexes: Strategies for a Winning Relationship*. Christian Faith Center. Seattle, Washington. 1964. 143 pgs.

Featured Products by Dr. C. Thomas and Pastor Maureen Anderson for Words for Winners

TAPE AND CD SERIES:

Laugh Your Way to Health
Understanding the Principles of Fasting & Prayer
Unleash the Power of Fasting and Prayer
Making Marriage a Love Story
How to be a Millionaire, God's Way
Profiles of the Rich and Famous
Untold Mysteries of the Holy Spirit
Conceptions and Misconceptions of the Holy Spirit

BOOKS:

Becoming a Millionaire God's Way
90 Days to Health
Making Impossibilities Possible
Confessing God's Word
Discovering The Power of Confession
Wisdom Wins
Wisdom Wins 2

These and many other books, tapes and CD's are available
from Living Word Bible Church. Order online at:

www.winners.tv

Or contact us at:
1-888-4WORDTV (1-888-496-7388), ext 118.